SCRIPTURAL
COUNSELING

SCRIPTURAL COUNSELING

A God-Centered Method

Oliver McMahan

CLEVELAND, TENNESSEE 37311

Library of Congress Catalog Card Number: 94-069939

ISBN: 0871489635

Copyright © 1995 by Pathway Press

Cleveland, Tennessee 37311

All Rights Reserved

Printed in the United States of America

Dedication

This book is loving dedicated to the arrows in my quiver (Psalm 127), Jonathan and Holly. They have been a joy and blessing. My prayer is that God will be the center and source of their lives.

Contents

PART I

The Roots of Pastoral Counseling

PART II

A God-Centered Method of Pastoral Counseling

PART III

The Application of Pastoral Counseling

Foreword

Based on the premise that "Christian counseling has a rich background in Scripture," this book charts the course of counseling from Old Testament times through New Testament principles into a modern application for pastoral ministry.

After surveying the general counseling movement and concurrent trends toward the methodological synthesis of both psychotherapy and theology, Oliver McMahan then systematically presents a scriptural strategy for pastoral counseling.

Drawing from his rich pastoral background in both the parish and clinical settings, Dr. McMahan sets forth a practical and yet sound God-centered counseling model which is true to both basic behavioral research and scriptural principles.

In these secular times when the Bible, as truth, is under fire and the basic tenets of humanism influence the modern counseling scene, *Scriptural Counseling* offers pastors and counseling practitioners at every level a Bible-based approach that opens up the counseling session for the ministry of the Holy Spirit in every phase of the process.

In the author's words: "God is the origination of the theocentric counseling. He sets the mold, parameters, and arrangement of the counseling. If anything godly occurs in counseling, it is first the result of His action and presence. He set the original goals and process in motion. Any godly accomplishment is the result of His intervention, though humans are involved in the process.

However, to maintain a God-centered perspective, the pastoral counselor and the counselee must confess that God was the origination of the process—the beginning—and the guiding presence and ending."

Paul L. Walker, Ph.D.
Senior Pastor
Mount Paran Church of God
Atlanta, Georgia

Acknowledgement

The concepts and practices in this volume reflect the input and fellowship of teachers, mentors, colleagues, parishoners, counselees, and students. Theocentricity is a process of relationships. Formation of God-centeredness in my counseling and ministry has involved individuals from all these sources.

In particular I would like to acknowledge the colleagues and students I have had the privilege to work with at the Church of God School of Theology and the Western School of Christian Ministry. Also, I would like to express gratitude for partners in ministry at Olive Branch Ministry of Mount Olive Church of God and Breakthough Counseling Institute, both in Cleveland, Tennessee.

Introduction

Pastoral counseling has been understood and practiced from various perspectives. The perspective of what works is certainly important; effectiveness is a vital concern. Maintaining a theological perspective is important because pastoral counseling is done in the context of Christian belief. Perspectives on pastoral counseling have also included the integration of various techniques, utilizing the best and most appropriate aspects of counseling approaches, choosing what might be best for the pastoral counseling setting.

The perspective of this volume addresses a number of vital concerns. These concerns include the following:

Scripture. To what degree does the Bible influence counseling? The Bible is the central document revealing the action of God in this world, providing the essential formation of pastoral counseling.

Center. Around what central criterion does pastoral counseling revolve? The central standard and barometer that guides and directs pastoral counseling is the action of God.

Origin. Where does the pastoral counseling begin and to what goal is our counsel directed? The ultimate beginning and final goal of the pastoral counseling process is found in the action of God.

Method. Behind every counseling method is a theory, and behind every counseling theory is a founder. Who is the founder, what is the essential theory, and to what degree does pastoral counseling reflect any particular theory and founder? The ultimate founder of pastoral counseling is God Pastoral counseling theory revolves around God and pastoral counseling methodology must consistently reflect God as founder and principal behind the process of pastoral counseling.

Applications. How can a God-centered method of counseling be applied to a variety of contemporary settings? Pastoral counseling can be applied to a variety of settings confronting individuals—crisis, stress, multiculturalism, and family.

Identity of the counselor. How does the pastoral counselor's self-identity relate to other helpers and counselors in the community? The pastoral counselor makes the distinctive contribution of focusong on individuals and problems from a God-centered perspective, thereby complementing others and maintaining one's own contribution as a God-centered counselor.

PART I

The Roots of Pastoral Counseling

Chapter 1

PASTORAL COUNSELING IN THE OLD TESTAMENT

Pastoral counseling is a vital part of ministry. It was practiced by the Old Testament saints. Jesus and the apostles also counseled people. The image of the shepherd/pastor incorporates wise counsel.

As important as it is in Scripture, counseling often bears a negative connotation. Some people equate counseling with humanism. It has been misinterpreted and criticized.

Some of the criticism is well deserved. Biblical concepts about counseling such as wisdom, righteousness, and holiness may have been lost in some cases. Counseling in the church does not always reflect a strong theology of the church. And some counselors may use methods that are not consistent with the scriptural presentation of counseling.

This book addresses the foundations, methods, and applications of pastoral counseling. Scripture is used as the primary source for insight and direction. While methodology is integrated, care has been taken to preserve the godly direction and precedents outlined in Scripture. The end result is a form of godly counsel consistent with Scripture and relative to the needs of individuals. The proposals in this book do not claim to be the only methods of godly counsel. However, they are consistent with scriptural principles, methods, and examples.

Part of the Shepherding Task

Ezekiel 34 and John 10 both present counseling as part of the shepherding task. These great, instructive passages about shepherding communicate the goals, direction, and methods of godly counsel. Shepherding can be seen as addressing the congregation as a whole. Pastoral counseling highlights the aspect of shepherding that ministers directly to individuals one-on-one.

The primary tasks of biblical shepherding and pastoring were protecting and nurturing the flock. Protecting meant to watch over and guard the sheep. Nurturing meant to provide food and nourishment for them. The protecting function is seen in the words of Jesus in John 10:11: "The good shepherd giveth his life for the sheep." Nurturing as a pastoral function is seen in Ezekiel 34. There the shepherds were judged because they fed themselves and not the sheep.

Counseling also involves both protecting and feeding. When individuals come for counsel, they are in a vulnerable position. Sin and/or suffering have taken their toll, causing them to fear that more peril threatens them. The pastoral counselor must guide the individual to a place of safety and rest. Individuals also come to a counselor in need of nourishment because their resources have run low and they have become weak. The counselor must provide refreshing ideas and tools for the nourishment of those they counsel.

Godly pastoral counseling does not ignore the human condition. Counsel is not a matter merely of ideas. Counseling principles provide necessary guidelines. However, counseling must use those ideas to provide care. People who come for counsel are usually hurting. The counselor does not help those in that condition by ignoring their real human needs. Their situation and condition must be analyzed, and counsel must address their needs.

These needs include spiritual, emotional, mental, behavioral, relational, and circumstantial issues. Each of these areas forms part of the human condition. People are created with an innate need for spiritual direction. Feelings are a vital part of the human experience. The capacity to think is God-given and is intended to be used for individuals' benefit and God's glory. Behavior must be addressed, for humans are creatures of action. Relationships are frequently a cause for anxiety in the counselee and must be addressed. Finally, the circumstances surrounding the individual must not be ignored.

Pastoral counseling is especially concerned with spiritual needs whether the counselee believes in Christ or not. Spiritual needs are related to all other areas of need. Spirituality is the foundation of care in Scripture. Though many other areas have been identified—for example, emotionality, cognition, and behavior—spiritual needs must also be addressed. Today, many counselors have removed or minimized the level of spiritual function in favor of other areas of need. Spirituality is considered by some as secondary or minimally applicable to a person's problems. However, pastoral counseling must consistently recognize the importance and central relevance of spirituality.

Examples of Counsel in Scripture

Scripture presents many examples of counseling. Counselors were seen as part of the shepherding function. Counseling was common in the courts of the kings. It was also part of the prophetic task. Isaiah reprimanded those who tried to counsel God. The disciples attempted to counsel Jesus at times. Ungodly counsel was sometimes given in parts of Scripture. All of these areas will be discussed in this book.

Much of the essence of counseling in Scripture is communicated by the Old Testament Hebrew term *ya'ats*. The term related to a two-way decision-making process. Examples included a political context (1 Kings 12:6), religious counsel (1 Kings 12:28), and counsel regarding worship (2 Chronicles 30:2). The emphasis was upon decision making. An individual would ask for counsel regarding a decision and would then participate with the counselor in that process.

Another important emphasis in scriptural counseling is communicated by the Old Testament term *etsah*. This term indicates a process in which the counselor gives more direct instruction and counsel. The person being counseled comes neither expecting nor needing a reciprocal exchange or relationship. Rather, direct answers and help are needed. Examples of this kind of counsel are especially seen when individuals sought counsel from the Lord (Joshua 9:14; Judges 18:5; 20:18, 23; 1 Samuel 14:37; 2 Samuel 16:23).

The Impact of Counseling on the People of God

The counseling ministry of the church and pastor is especially applied to those in need of the care of God. The focus of pastoral counseling is not upon the individual alone, the ability of the counselor to help people, or what the counselor and counselee may discover together. Instead, the focus of pastoral counseling is upon what an individual can receive from God. The function of the pastoral counselor is to aid in that process.

Pastoral counseling takes the dynamics of individual ministry and expands them to the body of believers. The counselor is aware and makes the counselee aware of the corporate nature of life. No one lives in isolation. Counsel is not given in a vacuum—separate and isolated. An individual is part of other relationships. The pastoral counselor highlights those relationships. Special attention is given to relationships formed in the home and the church family.

A particular function of pastoral counseling in the church is to bind the wounds of those who are in need of counsel. The pastoral counselor sees the church as the wounded community. Healing ministry in pastoral counseling may emphasize strength, power, and success. However, Scripture presents a greater emphasis upon the healing aspect of counsel within the body of believers. When someone seeks counsel within the church, it is usually to receive binding for wounds.

Another emphasis of pastoral counseling within the body of Christ is peril. When individuals come for counsel within the church, they are usually in peril because of an overwhelming need. They feel inadequate and alone. They are in a vulnerable position. Pastoral counseling emphasizes safety in the midst of danger and deliverance from peril.

Shepherding Others in Faithfulness to God

The Central Task of Shepherding

Pastoral counseling is strongly defined by the word *pastoral*. The term refers to the shepherding function. This task is described in both Testaments. This section looks at the definition in the Old Testament. This definition shapes the nature of pastoral counseling today.

The English word *shepherd* emphasizes "one who herds sheep." It means an individual who is with the sheep, guides them, and cares for them. The identity of the shepherd according to this description is rooted in the sheep.

The word *shepherd* in the Hebrew text is rooted in identity with feeding rather than with the sheep. The Hebrew word that is translated "shepherd" is *raah*—from the word for *feed*. The shepherd was known as "the one who feeds." This demonstrates that the shepherd's function was his most distinguishing characteristic.

The role of feeding required that the shepherd make a careful inspection of the terrain. Conditions in the Near East were extremely arid. Food was not always abundant. The shepherd had the responsibility of finding the pasture with the best food. This function was vital for the nourishment of the sheep.

The role of protecting the sheep was the second major function of the shepherd. In the ancient Near East, wild animals and thieves constantly posed a threat to the flock. Certain terrains and climates were also perilous to the flock. The shepherd had to constantly guard against these dangers. The watchfulness of the shepherd never ceased.

Protecting the flock also meant a measure of personal danger for the shepherd. The shepherd had to risk his life to protect the sheep. The dangers the sheep faced were also threats to the shepherd.

The peril of the unprotected flock is much more prominent in Scripture than the danger of an undernourished flock. If a shepherd neglected the flock, the flock would not starve. Rather, the more immediate peril was the danger faced by the flock. Some major examples in Scripture of the flock in peril are Ezekiel 34:5, 6; Matthew 9:36; and John 10.

God as the "Feeding One" and the Divine Shepherd

Some of the most meaningful insights about shepherding in the Old Testament come from the passages which describe God as the shepherd of His people. God cares for His people as a shepherd cares for his flock. This provides an example for the pastoral counselor.

In Genesis 48:15 Jacob declared that God had fed him all of his life. God, the sovereign Shepherd, also worked in the life of Joseph (Genesis 49:24). Though God's care for His people was depicted in many ways, the protection and care He gave was used in the metaphor of shepherding.

Just as the human shepherd watched over his flock, God gave protective oversight to His flock. The people of God are described as sheep because they continually depend upon the care of God. His care was the key to their nourishment and protection. They followed as He led them. They fed on the pasture He provided. They found rest and protection in the places He provided.

Being receptive to the shepherding of God brought many benefits to the people of God. They would not "want" or be "cut short" (Psalm 23:1). The feeding of the sheep was guaranteed (Psalm 37:3), and the flock came out from under God's care only if it rebelled against His leading. The rebellious flock is depicted in passages such as Numbers 27:14-17; 1 Kings 22:17; and 2 Chronicles 18:16.

The temperament and character of God's leading is seen in the themes of integrity, power, and gentleness. God shepherds His flock "according to the integrity of his heart" (Psalm 78:72). His leading does not depend purely on the circumstances surrounding the flock; He leads by His divine insight and loving mercy. He is both a powerful warrior and gentle shepherd (Isaiah 40:11). He has the power to cast down kingdoms while at the same moment carrying the young, tender, and weak in His bosom. God's provision is merciful, powerful, and tender as He shepherds His flock.

The Pastoral Counselor as a Shepherd of God's People

Pastoral counseling must be earmarked by the model of shepherding. Though the primary models patterned after secular notions of effect, cognition, and behavior provide insight into the pastoral counseling process, they do not provide a paradigm for pastoral counseling. The theme of shepherding provides a more biblically based understanding.

God has given divine provision to meet the demands of the shepherding task in counseling. The demands to care for and protect the flock may become overwhelming. Despite the failure of human shepherds, God still provides for His people as the divine Shepherd (Ezekiel 34:14-16; Hosea 4:16; Zechariah 11:4-7). Neither the counselor nor the counselee provide all that is needed for counseling therapy. The essential provision comes first and foremost from God. The pastoral counselor must depend on this divine provision.

God will judge the neglect, rebellion, and sin of those who fail to fulfill their calling to shepherd and counsel the people of God. Major passages covering this theme include Ezekiel 34; Zechariah 10:2, 3; 11:3-17; 13:7; Jeremiah 2:8; 10:21; 12:10; 22:22; 23:1-4; 25:34-36; 31:10; 50:6, 44; and 51:23.

In the passages above, shepherds neglected to carry out the responsibility that God had given to them. Examples of their failures include feeding themselves, instead of the sheep, devouring the sheep, failing to bring in those that had been driven away, failing to administer healing, and not guarding the sheep from danger. In these incidents, God responded by caring for the sheep through other means, including His personal intervention. At the same time, He administered judgment upon the shepherds. The moment of careful intervention for the sheep becomes a moment of decisive judgment for those who have failed to shepherd.

Those claiming to be pastoral counselors bear the mark and distinction of the shepherding metaphor. They are shepherds as they counsel. This is not merely another methodology or type of counseling. It is a ministry which God ordains and calls one unto. The implications of the calling place a divine responsibility upon the pastoral counselor.

In fulfilling the shepherding function, the pastoral counselor becomes a channel of God's promises. These shepherding promises are the same as the twofold shepherding function—to nourish and to protect.

God promises that the sheep will be fed and nourished. They may momentarily be in peril; nevertheless, the intervention of God guarantees the constant availability of nourishment. This is the theme of passages such as Psalm 37:3 and Numbers 27:16, 17.

God also promised the flock safe and restful pastures. These pastures were settings which represented the end result of the labor of the shepherd. The shepherd's task was to search out such places. Once the task was accomplished, the sheep could feed themselves. They would reap the rewards of the shepherd's labor. Texts which describe the task of finding pasture include Zephaniah 3:13; Psalm 23:2, 3; 65:12, 13.

Because of its special functions and responsibilities, the task of shepherding as a pastoral counselor must not be taken lightly. God uses shepherding to provide comfort, protection, and guidance for His people. He carries this function out in part through human shepherds. Since the shepherding task is a divine imperative, this aspect of pastoral counseling bears a distinct function and calling from God.

Teaching the Practice of Godly Wisdom: Wisdom and Counseling

Hebrew Concepts of Wisdom

Much of the counsel and advice given in Scripture is in the context of wisdom. The wise men of Scripture were similar to modern-day pastoral counselors. They were committed to providing insight from God's perspective. They were responsible for guiding the decisions and lifestyles of people in ancient Israel. Wisdom described goals for effective living.

Successful living was at the heart of the Hebrew concept of wisdom. Wisdom was not an abstraction; it was a very practical concept. It referred to a person's daily-life tasks, not to something dark and hidden from the understanding. God revealed wisdom to anyone who would receive and obey His counsel. Central to God's revelation of wisdom to individuals was His desire that they be effective in life. Wise counsel helped increase a person's effectiveness in living.

A wise man was one who knew how to do things well. He was not a person who merely dealt in abstractions, principles, or analyses. Just as a master craftsman used tools to create works of art for practical use, the wise man was skillful in the art of living (see Exodus 31:3, 4). He knew how to make decisions and to avoid pitfalls. He knew how to apply general rules and principles to the specifics of daily living. The wise man also knew how to effectively manage relationships. Whenever an individual wanted to know how to handle a critical situation, he sought out a wise man who would know how to skillfully master the situation.

One of the words often used for *wisdom* in the Old Testament was *chokmah,* which means dexterity and skill. The word referred to a person who had a proper grasp of the basic issues of life and who was in right relationship with God. Such a person was consistent in applying the wisdom of God to everyday living. Though the term referred to the discreet use of the mind, it did not refer to mere philosophy. It referred to the application of the mind to real life problems.

·Another key term used to refer to wisdom was the Hebrew word *biynah.* It emphasized understanding and insight. The ability to discern difficult situations was an important part of this skill. A wise man using this concept of wisdom would be able to judge between what was relevant and irrelevant for solving a difficult situation—and what was godly and ungodly.

A final Hebrew concept understood as wisdom was *tuwshiyah*. This term emphasized the sound and successful end result of wisdom. Wisdom from this perspective was something that could be relied upon—not a fanciful, untried possibility. It bore the mark of certainty that rested in God's revelation and insight. The wise man depended upon God's intervention and direction. This kind of wisdom was secure because of the acts of God, not the insight of individuals. This aspect of wisdom especially meant the ability to depend upon divine solutions for finite problems.

Those Identified as Wise

Various people in Scripture were identified as wise. These included members of royalty and persons of ability. Such royal figures as David and Solomon were recognized as being wise (1 Samuel 16:18; 2 Samuel 14:20; 1 Kings 2:6; 2 Chronicles 1:7-12). Persons of ability and success such as artisans and craftsmen also were called wise (Exodus 28:3; 31:3). The elderly were called wise because of their experience and ability in living (Job 12:12).

Individuals in Scripture who were called wise include Joseph, Moses, Daniel, and Deborah. In each of these instances, counsel was given to others. The basis of that counsel was not mere human insight, but wisdom gained through faithfulness to God.

Different Examples of Foolishness

The opposite of wisdom is foolishness. Foolishness is defined by several terms. One of these terms is *simple*. *Simple* is sometimes translated from the Hebrew word *pethiy*, which means one who is easily deceived. This is a person who has failed to responsibly use perception and discernment in life. The person is naive (Proverbs 14:15; 22:3), morally irresponsible (1:32), and aimlessly drifting without purpose (Proverbs 7).

"Fool" is the usual translation for the Hebrew term *keciyl,* which means dull or obstinate. The fool fails to respond to life's situations with wisdom. The emphasis is upon insensitivity to the demands and requirements of effective living. It was also used to indicate someone who had been spiritually insensitive (Proverbs 1:29-32). Such people were considered a menace to society (17:12).

Another Hebrew term sometimes translated as "fool" is *eviyl,* which means stubborn. A more indicting term than *keciyl,* it referred to an individual who had purposefully chosen to remain dull and unmoved by the prompting of wisdom (Proverbs 14:9).

The term usually translated "scorner" (KJV) or "scoffer" *(NKJV)* is *luwts.* The scoffer intentionally scorns wisdom. This type of foolishness is marked by sarcasm and a strong dislike for correction (Proverbs 9:7, 8; 13:1; 15:12). The scoffer may be a deliberate trouble-maker, causing trouble at random (21:24; 22:10; 29:8). He is a bad influence upon others (24:9). At times, the Lord gave the scoffer some of the pain he had given others (3:34).

A final description of foolishness was captured in the term *sluggard,* which indicated someone who would not do what was necessary for effective living (Proverbs 6:9, 10). He would not finish what was necessary (12:27). The sluggard would even fail to face the things pertinent to wise living (20:4; 22:13; 26:16). Finally, because of the frustration created by foolish living, the sluggard was continually restless (13:4; 21:25, 26).

Teaching the Practice of Wisdom

One of the most important aspects of Hebrew wisdom was the model of the wise counselor. The counselor, or wise man, was not merely an adviser concerning things he had not accomplished himself. On the contrary, it was required that the counselor exemplify wisdom in his own life. Wisdom was not a mere abstraction. It was a lifestyle. The modeling of this lifestyle was an important part of the wise man's counsel.

The most significant aspect of the modeling process was dependency on God. The wise man's faith in God had to shine forth more than any other aspect of his life. He was not necessarily a perfect person. Although he was very capable in life, this was not equated with perfection. However, faith would be an absolute requirement for the wise counselor.

The pastoral counselor today must use the concepts communicated in the Wisdom Literature of Scripture. These books include Job, Psalms, Proverbs, and Ecclesiastes. When the Old Testament speaks of counsel, it is from the perspective of wisdom. The purpose of the books on wisdom was to give counsel to the people of God. Though many precepts are found in other portions of Scripture, the most direct source for counseling information is the Wisdom Literature.

Solomon and Pastoral Counseling

Choosing the Priority of Wisdom

As mentioned in the previous section, a major foundation of pastoral counseling is wisdom. This biblical concept is illustrated in the call of Solomon, the wisest of the wise counselors of Israel. The foundational call he experienced in 1 Kings 3 informs us about the nature of wisdom and counseling. This section will look at the calling of Solomon as an illustration of biblical principles that apply to pastoral counseling.

The Context of Worship (1 Kings 3:1-4)

Solomon built his empire upon godly wisdom granted directly from God. It is very important to note that Solomon's wisdom came from God and was not the result of human ingenuity. Solomon's story is not a glorification of wisdom but a celebration of God's wisdom as it was sought after by the young ruler. Wisdom and insight in pastoral counseling does not originate with the counselor, the counselee, or their relationship but is granted by God. Reliance on Him is the beginning of insight in pastoral counseling.

In the first part of 1 Kings 3, Solomon worshiped God in high places. He was sincere, but he mixed his worship with idolatry. Solomon had an encounter with the Lord that addressed Solomon's need for complete obedience, the need for a central place of worship in Jerusalem, and the need for a godly foundation for Solomon's growing empire. This encounter moved Solomon to purify his worship and establish a godly foundation for his life.

In the midst of Solomon's worship and sacrifice, the Lord came to him in a dream. The significance of Solomon's encounter with the Lord is twofold. It is a recognition of the importance of worship. The dream and request began in the context of worship and ended with a worshipful response (v. 15).

However, the second and greater significance of Solomon's encounter with the Lord is that it transformed his worship. He no longer worshiped in the high places but in the proper place, before the ark of the Lord.

Solomon was affected by worship as he faced the issues of life. His encounter with the Lord gave him wisdom and transformed his worship. His worship was at the heart of his wisdom.

Wisdom is fostered in the context of worship; it also transforms worship. Sometimes wisdom and worship are set apart and seen as polarizations one against the other. However, they are interrelated. In fact, worship makes the reception of wisdom from God possible.

The foundation of faithfulness in worship is at the heart of wisdom and pastoral counseling. Worship is an integral part of pastoral counseling.

Solomon's Foundation for Wisdom (1 Kings 3:5, 6)

Solomon's wisdom was founded in God's mercy. Solomon recognized the great mercy God had already extended to him and his father. God had allowed Solomon, David's son, to rise to power. Solomon called it a kindness. In the Hebrew text, the word for *kindness* is *checed,* the same word used earlier for *mercy.* It means love and mercy demonstrated especially by faithfulness. Solomon recognized that God had been faithful in His love and mercy.

Solomon's Recognition of His True Need (1 Kings 3:7-9)

Solomon was aware of the relationship of faithfulness between David and the Lord. And he realized that if he was to have the faithfulness of the Lord to continue in his life, he would have to demonstrate his faithfulness to God also.

Realizing the importance of his personal faithfulness to God, Solomon confessed his need rather than what he might gain. Solomon exhibited the very qualities he had mentioned about his father, David. He humbly confessed his personal inadequacies in this statement: "I am but a little child." The Hebrew word translated "child" is *naar*. The word actually means young man or youth.

Solomon defined his youthfulness and personal needs in two ways. First, he recognized his inability to know the way "to go out or come in"—a reference to decision making and discerning between issues. Second, He recognized the great task of leading the multitude of people for whom he was responsible.

In the midst of the recognition of his needs, Solomon demonstrated his faithfulness to the Lord as well. He recognized that he had become king only because the Lord had made him so (v. 7). He confessed that the people he was now responsible to lead were God's chosen people (v. 8). Solomon's sense of need was not only for his personal needs but also for the tremendous responsibility given him by God.

The importance of a task and the assessment of our need should be not only for physical concerns but also for the reverence and godliness required by God. Sensing God's direction and His requirements in the midst of a task produces the kind of humility displayed by Solomon in this passage. Solomon felt certain needs because of the responsibility God had placed upon him. He was not looking toward what he might gain.

Solomon's choice for godly wisdom was based upon his recognition that the nation was God's. In light of this fact, Solomon asked for an understanding heart, the ability to judge, and the ability to discern between good and bad.

The heart of Solomon's request centered on the ability to discern (*biyn*) and thereby judge (*shaphat*). The means by which this was accomplished was understanding (*shama*) in Solomon's heart.

The Hebrew word *biyn,* translated "discern" in verses 9 and 11 and "understanding" in verse 12, emphasizes the ability to make an assessment and distinguish between what is right and wrong, or godly and ungodly.

The Hebrew *shaphat,* translated "judge" in verse 9, emphasizes the ability to administer that which would be upright according to God's standard.

The emphasis of discernment is upon the ability to distinguish between the issues of a question. The emphasis of judgment is upon the maintenance of God's standard regarding a question. Solomon asked for a heart capable of doing both.

It is important to note that Solomon sought these qualities because of his desire to accomplish the purposes of God, not because he was infatuated with wisdom. Solomon did not want simply to be wise and just; he wanted to fulfill the purposes God had set for him as king of the nation.

The key to Solomon's wisdom is captured in the word *give.* His capacity to lead the people in wisdom was not the result of his ingenuity but because God had given him wisdom.

Godly wisdom is revealed wisdom. The primary way in which God reveals His wisdom today is the Scriptures. It is the standard by which to judge all that is claimed to be wise. Another method God uses is the counsel of godly men and women who are led by the Spirit of God. Further, God uses the witness of His Spirit to instruct and lead His people.

Pleasing God (1 Kings 3:10-12)

The word *pleased* in verse 10 indicates that it was

"good to the eyes" of the Lord. The emphasis is upon the delight Solomon's choice brought to the Lord. Wisdom itself is a noble virtue, but the greatest aspect of Solomon's choice is that it pleased the Lord. God's standard was the ultimate criterion by which Solomon's choice was judged.

Verses 11 and 12 indicate the reason Solomon's choice pleased God. Solomon did not request things that would have brought him personal gain. The self-serving things Solomon did not choose were longevity, riches, and the destruction of his enemies. When selfish gain is chosen over godly discernment and wisdom, it usually means a false assumption about longevity, a lust for wealth, and a desire to see others destroyed. A choice to obey the commands of God and seek godly wisdom is also a choice to deny oneself in order to serve God.

God granted Solomon the wise heart he had requested. The Hebrew term translated "wise" (*chakam*) means the ability to carry out the judgments of God. This ability was part of the request in verse 9. God also gave Solomon a discerning heart. That God granted Solomon a heart that was understanding, discerning (*biyn*), and wise means he could discern good and evil in difficult situations and maintain the just standards of the Lord whenever he made critical decisions.

Wisdom as God's Blessing (1 Kings 3:13, 14)

God gave Solomon the things for which he had not asked because of the condition of his heart. Now that Solomon had shown a spirit of humility and obedience, the Lord decided to grant him also the riches and honor he did not choose.

Riches, honor from others, or longevity are not evil unless they are elevated above God. The fact that

Solomon had not requested them but had rather sought godly judgment and wisdom indicated that he served God and not riches, honor from others, or long life.

God wants first place in the hearts of all His people. Without this priority, blessings that He bestows upon them can become the means for self-serving and evil corruption. The God of the blessing—not the content of a potential blessing—should be the focus of a Christian's desire.

Applying Wisdom in the Context of Pastoral Counseling

In 1 Kings 3:16-28, Solomon provided a paradigm for wisdom in pastoral counseling. Solomon's personal encounter with God predicated his wisdom. God rewarded Solomon's faithfulness by giving him godly wisdom. The wisdom required in the pastoral counseling process is also based upon personal faithfulness before God. The attributes that Solomon displayed and the rewards of wisdom that God granted serve as an illustration of the dynamics required in pastoral counseling today.

Solomon's wisdom was tested when two mothers both claimed to be the true mother of an infant. Both women were of questionable reputation; they were harlots. Their stories were in direct conflict. The mothers both claimed the other woman had switched a dead child for the living one. And to further complicate matters, there were no witnesses. What judgment would uphold the standards of God's justice and properly discern between the two women?

Solomon's final decision would reveal that the wisdom God had given Solomon was truly great. It was based on truth and justice. Further, it probed the inner motivations of those involved. Solomon's wisdom probed beyond the external circumstances of the case and into the internal witness of each mother's heart. He did this by raising the issue of the death of the surviving infant. The final judgment was decisive because not only was it the result of his assessment, but it also reflected the inner motivation of the two women.

When Solomon posed the question by threatening the life of the child, he was applying the wisdom God had given him. He was able to discern not only between truth and error but also between the good and evil within hearts.

The real mother of the infant, driven by the love of her heart for her child, was willing to sacrifice spending her life with the child in order to spare its life. Solomon saw this love as proof of her motherhood and quickly declared it in verse 27.

The conclusion of verse 28 is extremely important in seeing the truth of Solomon as a paradigm for pastoral counselors. What the nation saw in Solomon's wisdom was God, not Solomon's ability or Solomon himself.

The people were greatly impressed by Solomon, but the reason was not Solomon himself or his judgments. They recognized that his wisdom came from the Lord whom Solomon served. The wisdom he used was God-centered—coming from God and centering on God.

Suggestions for Application

The concepts of pastoral counseling must not remain in an "ivory tower" far removed from the needs of individuals. To apply the principles discussed in this chapter, the following are suggested:

1. Consider establishing a place for a ministry of pastoral counseling in the local church. It can be part of the pastor's ministry or a separate staff position.

2. Develop established principles of counseling in pastoral ministry. While there are many ideas that are distributed in counseling literature, pastors need to decide individually what principles will serve as a guide in their own ministry.

3. Communicate principles of care and compassion through worship and preaching experiences. The principles of suffering, healing, binding, and receiving ministry on an individual basis must be known by all people in the church body.

4. Develop a section on pastoral counseling in your ministry library. These will serve as references when individuals come for help and assistance.

5. Prepare a brochure and/or pamphlet which clarifies the shepherding function as part of the ministry of pastoral counseling.

6. Communicate the shepherding of God in the midst of the pastoral counseling process. Remind the counselee that God is vitally involved in the midst of therapy.

7. Share the burden of shepherding with fellow shepherds. The task of being a pastoral counselor can be overwhelming. God may use another shepherd to pastor you.

8. Use principles and illustrations from Scripture which remind counselees of the impact the shepherding metaphor has made upon your concept of pastoral counseling.

9. Use the books of Wisdom Literature as homework assignments. Ask counselees to find principles which apply to their situation.

10. Focus on the central concept of faithfulness at the heart of wisdom. Wisdom is not merely a rational or cognitive exercise. It is an extension of one's faith in God.

11. Use the concepts of the wise person and the fool to categorize responses to God's call to faithfulness. Profiling these characters in Scripture provides examples for counselees.

12. Select certain themes, such as finance, and trace their application in the Wisdom Literature. Many topics are not clearly organized in sections and may require organizing by the counselor in order to apply them.

13. Make worship a vital part of the pastoral counseling process. Implement it as a regular step in your methodology.

14. Look for character as much as problem behavior. Character is the ultimate goal of wisdom.

15. Enter into the process of worship with the counselee. This allows God to grant wisdom to you as the counselor as much as to the counselee.

16. Make the application of wisdom as much a process of internal focus on the heart as external focus upon circumstances and relationships.

Chapter 2

PASTORAL COUNSELING IN THE NEW TESTAMENT

Counseling was an important part of Jesus' ministry. He frequently ministered to the masses, but much of His ministry was directed toward individuals. The ministry of Jesus one-on-one with individuals can be viewed as pastoral counseling ministry. His counseling dynamics can be observed in encounters with the sick, the possessed, the troubled, and the poor.

A central aspect of Christ's ministry to individuals can be seen in His suffering. Isaiah 53 especially develops the theme of compassion. Christ's passion for ministry, even counseling ministry, to individuals is expressed in terms of burden bearing and suffering. The Cross is the pivotal event describing Christ's care and suffering for individuals.

Jesus' Ministry as Shepherd

Jesus provides the strongest paradigm for pastoral counseling in the New Testament. At the heart of the paradigm is His function as the Chief Shepherd of the believer. The metaphor of *shepherd* captures the care He used in ministry. This shepherding care is illustrated in His teaching on being a shepherd. One of Jesus' strongest teachings on the subject is recorded in John 10.

The Guarding Shepherd (vv. 8, 9)

The first essential aspect of shepherding Jesus addressed was protecting. In the description of Old Testament themes for pastoral counseling in the previous chapter, protecting was discussed as a major function. Jesus emphasized this same function: "All that ever came before me are thieves and robbers: but the sheep did not hear them. I am the door: by me if any man enter in, he shall be saved, and shall go in and out, and find pasture" (John 10:8, 9).

This passage identifies the importance of protection. The shepherd is the door, standing between the sheep and danger. The shepherd is responsible for the welfare of the sheep. The latter part of verse 9 indicates that protection naturally facilitates nourishment. However, without sound protection, feeding is not possible.

The pastoral counselor needs to be aware of the vulnerability of the counselee. Individuals come for counseling when they are weak. They may be very discouraged. They usually come with a strong need. The counselor needs to respond, feeling a reasonable amount of responsibility for the welfare and oversight of the individual.

The Nurturing Shepherd (v. 10)

Jesus emphasized the shepherd's nurturing function by first contrasting the lack of nourishment. If the shepherd did not properly feed the sheep, they would be prey to the thief. The thief did not care for the nurture of the sheep. His goal was to destroy the sheep. There is little neutrality in this passage. Either the sheep were being nourished or they were prey. Consequently, without proper nurture, the counselee is subject to become prey to relationships and circumstances that are not edifying. He can become susceptible to harmful forces.

The shepherd provided abundant resources for the sheep. Not only was there provision for sustenance, there was a surplus of provision. This ensured the quality of care for the sheep. One of the eventual goals of the counselor is to see the counselee thrive, flourish, and experience abundant life.

Presence of God as God (v. 38)

Jesus climaxed His description of the shepherding function by declaring His deity and presence. After being ridiculed and criticized by the Pharisees for teaching on shepherding, Jesus declared that He was the divine Messiah. This assured believers that the One who shepherded them was God.

The presence of God is at the heart of the pastoral counseling process. Just as the presence of the shepherd gave comfort to the sheep, the divine presence of God gives encouragement and guidance to a counselee. The pastoral counselor must learn to foster an awareness of God's presence in the midst of the counseling process.

Jesus' Ministry as Healer

Jesus' ministry as healer provides another insight for pastoral counseling. Two Greek terms describe the healing ministry of Jesus. *Therapeuo* emphasized the personal care of Christ's healing process. *Iaomai* emphasized the life-giving process of His healing. Both concepts instruct the pastoral counselor today. The process of pastoral counseling gives the counselee assurance and support. It also offers newness of life. These concepts demonstrate that Christ's healing was a complete and effective process.

Pastoral Counseling as Service (*Therapeuo*)

Matthew 4:23, 24 describes the manner in which Jesus went through many places healing the sick. The term indicating healing in these verses is therapeuo, which came from a root concept meaning "to serve." The emphasis of the term was the tender, serving, and compassionate care of the Master in the healing process. This does not detract from the fact that actual, physical miracles were done. It enhances the meaning of these events by highlighting the loving and caring manner in which Christ served as he healed. The pastoral counselor also should temper his work with thoughtful, serving care and concern. Jesus demonstrated that service and care during the counseling process is just as important as the end result.

The healing of Mary Magdalene from evil spirits emphasized Christ's care. This woman was converted and delivered by Christ's ministry. She became a close follower of the Lord and was the first to proclaim His resurrection. The power to deliver her from oppressive and binding spirits was real. Dealing with demonic power is a very difficult process. Despite the pressure, however, Jesus still served with loving care. The pastoral counselor must not be pressured by the complexity and stressful nature of a counselee's problems, but must maintain a loving focus upon the individual's need for care.

Pastoral Counseling as Cure (*Iaomai*)

A second term which provides insight into pastoral counseling is *iaomai*. This term indicates healing which brings a cure and life. It highlights the effective changes that took place as a result of Christ's one-on-one ministry. When Jesus administered His healing power, changes took place in the lives of individuals. In a similar manner, the pastoral counselor must be confident of the power of God to make a difference in a counselee's life. The pastoral counselor does not merely offer an alternative approach to life. Instead, he presents an answer rooted in God's own work. That work is powerful and will change an individual's life.

The disease and conditions Jesus addressed were very serious. They were real perils threatening those in need of ministry. The power of the change that took place was greater than any peril faced by them. The healing and change Christ brought about ministered to the person's area of greatest need. This was effective power which overcame the perils they faced.

Some Ways Jesus Encountered People in Ministering His Care

Nicodemus—the Reality of New Life (John 3)

Jesus' response to Nicodemus provides a model for pastoral counseling assessment. Jesus did not ignore needs in Nicodemus' life. Jesus carefully but definitely addressed Nicodemus' condition. He was straightforward in making Nicodemus aware of his need. Nicodemus came with certain inquiries about his condition. Jesus addressed some of those concerns. However, Jesus assessed Nicodemus' needs from a spiritual perspective. Though the pastoral counselor is not to spiritualize every area of life, a spiritual assessment provides central guidance in addressing areas of need in a counselee's life.

Jesus essentially offered Nicodemus newness of life. This proposal placed responsibility upon Nicodemus to be open to the work of God. God was offering the gift of life to Nicodemus. It was now incumbent upon him to accept or reject this proposal. In a similar sense, the pastoral counselor provides answers and solutions that will bring newness to the life of an individual. The counselor should clarify the responsibility of the counselee to accept or reject the work of God in his life.

Woman Guilty of Adultery— Empowered by Forgiveness (John 8:1-11)

In John 8:1-11, Jesus' response to the woman caught in adultery provides an example for pastoral counseling responses. There were those who were ready to condemn the woman without offering any reconciliation or care for her. Jesus responded truthfully, yet lovingly, and ministered to her. Though He did not deny the reality of her sinful condition, He offered her complete deliverance from the weight of her guilt.

When Jesus initially encountered the woman, He did not highlight the judgment that rested upon her. The passage indicates that she was indeed guilty. Jesus' nonjudgmental response placed responsibility for judging the woman with the heavenly Father. His focus was upon care and ministry. Similarly, the pastoral counselor must respond to individuals, confident of the Father's judgment and open to His corresponding call to minister in love.

Jesus expressed an important skill that pastoral counselors must learn. This skill is to compassionately respond to a needy, even sinful, individual without condoning sinful behavior. Jesus identified the fact that she had sinned but did not make that the focus of His ministry. His focus was upon leading the woman to a reconciling relationship with the heavenly Father. Pastoral counselors are ineffective by merely focusing upon individuals' needs and sins. Instead they should focus upon the development of a godly relationship between the counselee and God the Father.

Jesus offered the woman tangible help. He gave instructions which extended beyond their time together. As she left, He admonished her to discontinue her sinful life. This demonstrated His concern for her and that He was not just interested in temporary solutions. He clarified ongoing needs in her life and then assigned her the responsibility for maintaining what had been accomplished. Pastoral counselors need to clarify the responsibilities that counselees have beyond the counseling hour. Counseling should address these extended concerns just as forcefully as any dynamics that may occur during the actual counseling session.

Jesus' compassionate model as shepherd sets the tone for the kind of care pastoral counselors should offer. The effectiveness of Jesus' care challenges pastoral counselors to press for real solutions to the dilemmas people face when they come for counseling. Jesus' skill in compassion without condoning sin sets the pace for a realistic yet redeeming approach to pastoral counseling today.

Submitting Yourselves in the Fear of God—
The Counseling of Paul

The counseling ministry of Paul can be observed

through the principles he presented in his epistles. In his letters he wrote of individuals to whom he ministered on a one-on-one basis. Paul also addressed the churches as a group. In the dynamics he communicated, there are many applications to personality and group development. His concerns for discipleship and Christian maturity reflect his compassion for ministry. This compassion forms an essential paradigm for pastoral counseling. This chapter will consider one of the most thorough sections presented by Paul on human behavior in the church—Ephesians 4 and 5.

Discipleship as a Vital Part of the Context of the Church (Ephesians 4:11, 12)

In formulating principles for ministry to those in need, Paul firmly communicated the importance of the church. The ministry that Paul had with individuals as well as with groups was rooted in his concept of the church. Ministry to individuals was synonymous with ministry in the church. By implication, Christian counseling must enhance the ministry of the church. Pastoral counseling is not a task independent from the church. Paul did not separate the two.

Paul defined the church as a place where God provided gifts and abilities to meet the needs of those who came. These were provisions from God and not the natural abilities of individuals. God's enabling power was central. Care was provided for those in the church because of the care that God had given. He had given gifts and offices to the church so that needs would be met.

Paul taught the essential goal of "perfecting" the saints (v. 12). To perfect is to equip an individual for the tasks involved in life and ministry. The concept came from a root term which meant "to be fitted." It was a masonry term which described a brick or stone that was properly cut to fit in a designated place and be functional in that place. The work of the church, and consequently pastoral counseling, is to equip individuals for life and ministry. This process is a "cutting" and "fitting" for the demands placed upon them.

Primacy of Love in Communication and Relationships (Ephesians 4:15)

Another major subject of Paul in Ephesians was communication. He was concerned that the goal of equipping the believer would be hindered by a lack of godly communication. Communication is an important facilitator in the process of equipping. Life skills and tasks cannot be accomplished without an effective strategy for communicating.

Paul emphasized the content of communication with his use of the word *truth* in verse 15. It referred to the accuracy and boundaries of information and relationships. Ultimately, the standard of truth is God and His Word. Communication must be accurate.

Paul also emphasized the context in which truth was to be communicated. Regardless of the accuracy of the information, it must be communicated in love. Without this context, communication becomes ungodly and ineffective. This twofold focus of communication is very important. The ultimate example is God, who sent the Truth—His Son—in love unto the world.

Important Aspects of Godly Relationships (Ephesians 4:25-32)

Paul specified various aspects of relationship which are

built on the foundation of godly communication—speaking the truth in love. These aspects represent various ways in which behavior, attitudes, and thinking reflect godly communication. Paul was committed to instructing the Ephesians about these specifics in living.

Christian counselors must be committed to specific applications of Christian principles of relationship. Principles such as speaking the truth in love are important. However, they are ineffective unless they are specifically applied to everyday living. That application can be difficult for counselees to make without assistance.

The Primacy of Truth in Relationships

Paul emphasized the necessity of truth in relationships. In verse 25 he admonished the people to put away lying. He encouraged them to adopt a lifestyle of genuineness and truth. Then he gave the underlying, practical reason for this commitment. They were in a bond of close relationship. This bond meant they had to function together, not separately. They were knit together in love. This made it incumbent upon them to work together in harmony and truth. Without this level of genuine relationships, they could not function effectively together or as individuals.

The Call to Monitor Anger and Emotions in Relationships

Paul also appealed to the Ephesians to monitor their emotions for greater faithfulness and effectiveness. He especially focused upon anger (v. 26, 27) and admonished them not to allow their anger to persist. Prolonged anger creates problems for the individual and the group.

It also provides the opportunity for sin. This principle applies to emotions in general. The Christian counselor must address emotions and equip counselees to monitor their emotions.

Accepting Proper Personal Responsibility in Relationships

In verse 28, Paul instructed the church about responsibility. He recognized that every believer has a sphere of obligations that include employment, relationships, and assignments within the church. Stealing would be to take as theirs something that belonged to someone else. This was not right. Instead, they were to work within the scope of their responsibilities and not manipulate the benefits of the labors of others. Christian counselors must equip counselees in assuming responsibility for their own actions.

Using Communication Which Edifies in Relationships

Edifying communication was another behavior addressed by Paul (v. 29). Communicating in love meant that others were to be built up by one's communication. "Corrupt communication" was a phrase used by Paul to indicate that which tears down another person. Godly communication increases the potential and condition of others. Christian counselors must develop approaches which assist counselees in developing edifying communication.

Central Focus Upon the Holy Spirit in Relationships

In summarizing behavior, Paul emphasized sensitivity to the Holy Spirit (v. 30). The specific application of the behaviors discussed relied upon the guidance of the Holy

Spirit. The Spirit directs believers when to communicate and in what manner to communicate. He also guides emotions and clarifies spheres of responsibility. Grieving the Holy Spirit is the initial act that misdirects behavior. This conveys the eternal and divine implications of a person's actions. The Christian counselor must highlight the centrality of the guidance of the Holy Spirit in directing a person's behavior.

Kindness Demonstrated in the Context of Forgiveness in Relationships

A final emphasis of Paul in this section on specific behaviors is forgiveness (vv. 31, 32). This attitude reflects the underlying foundation for relationships. If there is a violation of relationships, individuals should be willing to ask forgiveness and/or forgive others. This admits the imperfect nature of the human condition and maintains the promise of improvement. It is an interpersonal means of edification. Christian counselors should use forgiveness as a catalyst for godly behavior and a bond for the maintenance of those behaviors.

Primacy of Submitting One to Another (Ephesians 5:21)

In summarizing much of what he said about godly attitudes, behavior, and relationships, Paul emphasized the role of submission. This emphasis comes in the latter portion of Ephesians 5. Submission is a central concept he illustrated with marital relationships. Submission is the expression of a Spirit-filled life (v. 18). It is one of the most critical factors in effective relationships.

The word translated "submitting" is from a Greek

word which emphasizes placing oneself under another. It depicts the admission of the status of another individual. This attitude guards against abuse toward another person and maintains respect for that person. The emphasis is upon regard for another individual's position and potential. The opposite of this condition is hatred and malice toward another. The distinctive characteristic of submission is commitment to the status of another. Christian counselors must equip counselees in clarifying the status of others and then being submissive in relationships.

The motivation for submitting to others is faithfulness to God. Paul instructed that there should be mutual submission and that it must be "in the fear of God" (v. 21). The inherent value of another individual is not the essential motivation. People are valuable and worthy. Positions may be venerable and honorable. However, the importance of the individual does not begin with the individual; it comes from God. As a result, submission is an act of faith, not a mere affirmation of human potential or position. This God-centered focus and motivation should be a strong emphasis of the Christian counselor.

Edifying One Another: Counsel in the New Testament Church

A review of the relational dynamics encouraged in the early church can give insight into the criteria they used in counseling. The New Testament church was vitally concerned about relationships. Both the Book of Acts and the Epistles give descriptions of one-on-one confrontations and exhortations. These occasions of counseling were guided by certain criteria for relationships.

Observing these criteria provides insight into the counseling of the New Testament church.

This section will focus upon the terms used by the New Testament to describe types of relationships. The phrase "one another" was used in the Epistles and Acts to refer to relationships. Certain attributes were used in connection with this phrase to define relationships. These attributes included qualities both to develop and to avoid. This section will look at the occurrences of the phrase "one another" and the relational dynamics surrounding its use. Relational terms used with the phrase form the basis of this analysis of pastoral counseling goals for today.

All of these concepts set the tone for edifying one another. Christ said that believers' love for one another would be the witness that they were His disciples (John 13:34, 35). The ministry of the church sought to center believer's relationships in God.

Positive Attributes to Develop in Godly Relationships

Kind affection emphasizes love and tenderness in relationships. The term is from the Greek word *philostorgos*, which is a combination of two Greek words—*love* and *affection.* This means that the tendency of an individual is prone toward love. A believer is to have a lifestyle tempered toward affection and tenderness. In Romans 12:10 this concept is used for having kind affection to one another in relationships.

Love emphasizes love directed by God. It is the result of the use of intelligence and comprehension, but it is centered upon the purposes of God. The term used in the Greek text is *agape.* This love does not indicate mere affection. This love seeks higher purposes than mere emotions. Emotions may be felt, but the focus of love is a central meaning and motivation. For believers this is love. In relating to one another, their love is from God. Believers are admonished to love one another in relationships (Romans 13:8; 1 Thessalonians 4:9; 1 Peter 1:22; 1 John 3:11, 23; 4:7, 11; 2 John 5).

Receive emphasizes acts of kindness and love. It is the translation of the Greek term *proslambano*. The word was used in contexts of action. In the New Testament context, individuals demonstrated kindness by bringing someone to their house and receiving them as an equal. By these acts they would be drawing closer, "receiving" the person. This term is used for receiving one another in relationships (Romans 15:7). The opposite was to either remain at a distance or pull further away from an individual.

Admonish is translated from *noutheteo*, which is made up of two Greek terms, *nous* (mind/will) and *tithemi* (to place). It emphasizes the presentation of something to another person and means that a thought, concept, or principle is placed in front of, or in the mind of, the person. The term does not emphasize the creation of anything. Rather, something already created is brought to another person. Fellow Christians are to bring to others' attention things important for them to know and consider, especially the things of God. This term is used for admonishing one another in relationships (Romans 15:14).

Salute and *greet* emphasize the importance of gestures of affection. As with *receive*, the focus is action. Affection is communicated through tangible actions—gestures of kindness and warmth, such as a kiss or embrace. These actions are necessary to give assurance and support to a relationship. The Greek term used for this concept, *aspazomai*, which has the sense of union and was used for saluting and greeting one another in relationships (Romans 16:16; 1 Corinthians 16:20; 2 Corinthians 13:12; 1 Peter 5:14).

Serve—translated from *douleo*, the Greek word for bond servant—emphasizes service and commitment to one another. Action is important. The feelings and affections a person has toward another must be communicated through appropriate and edifying acts of service. These acts frequently relate to the physical and temporal needs of an individual. The term is used regarding relationships in which commitment and service are very important. This concept for serving one another in relationships is used in Galatians 5:13.

Forbear emphasizes characteristics that sustain a relationship. The term stresses the need for resilience and flexibility in a relationship. Various actions and attitudes such as forgiveness, love, and endurance may be used. However, this term emphasizes the overall need to remain committed to a relationship over an extended period of time. This aspect of forbearing one another in relationships is highlighted in Ephesians 4:2 and Colossians 3:13.

Kindness emphasizes a gracious and pleasant attitude. "Be ye kind one to another," Paul instructed in Ephesians 4:32. The word *kind* is translated from the Greek word *chrestos*, which means offering kindness and assistance. The opposite is be to be harsh and withhold help. A person with an attitude of kindness is sensitive to the needs of others and willing to help them If someone needs something a person has, there is little hesitance to lend aid. The term is used here for being kind to one another in relationships.

Forgive emphasizes a willingness to give favor and forgiveness to someone. It is translated from the Greek word *charizomai*. The first part of the word is from *charis*, the same root as *grace*. Its meaning is rooted in the idea of graciousness. It means to respond with favor toward others who may or may not request it. This quality does not condone evil or wrongdoing. However, a person with this quality has a forgiving/grace-giving spirit and is open to relating to individuals. Forgiving one another in relationships is mentioned in Ephesians 4:32 and Colossians 3:13.

Comforting and *consoling* emphasize a comforting presence offered to someone else. The term in the Greek text is *parakaleo*, a combination of two Greek terms, *para* (alongside of) and *kaleo* (to call). It means to call someone to your side. It is comfort that comes by virtue of the presence of another individual. That person may do a lot of things to help another person. However, the most helpful aspect of the relationship is the presence and availability of the other person. Comforting one another in relationships is emphasized in 1 Thessalonians 4:18 and 5:11.

Edify means to build up another person to improve the quality of life. Those who edify others are not directed by selfish or manipulative motives. They help to develop someone else through a godly attitude, effective organization, and timely action. Edifying one another is used regarding relationships in 1 Thessalonians 5:11.

Consider, from the Greek term *katanoeo,* emphasizes perception and understanding. It describes the cognitive process of applying the mind and will to relationships. Rather than merely reacting to others, thoughtful consideration of options, circumstances, and implications for relationships is important. Considering one another in relationships is used in Hebrews 10:24.

Negative Aspects to Avoid in Godly Relationships

Negative aspects to avoid were also used in references to relationships in the early church. These admonitions also provide insight into principles about relationships that guided the counsel and ministry of the early church.

Judging emphasizes a judgmental attitude that presumes upon the final authority of God. The New Testament affirms the sovereign will and judgment of God. No individual is to act as though he is the final authority regarding relationships. We should make assessments and be wise and discerning. However, conclusions are always humbly subjected to the judgment of God. Judging one another is applied to relationships in Romans 14:13.

Devouring emphasizes a self-centered attitude. This kind of spirit seeks to take advantage of others and relationships. Self-fulfillment is the sole purpose for relating to others. Devouring one another is applied to relationships in Galatians 5:15.

Consuming emphasizes the perpetual desire to merely devour something in a severe way. It is different from *devour* in its duration. To consume is a continual, habitual condition in relationships. Consuming one another is applied to relationships in Galatians 5:15.

Provoking emphasizes a challenging and combative spirit that thrives on conflict and feels that conflict is necessary. This kind of person is not satisfied until some controversy is started in relationships. Provoking one another is applied to relationships in Galatians 5:26.

Envying emphasizes jealousy. It refers to a selfish desire for something possessed by another person. The implications of envy can be destructive. An envious person may go to extremes in trying to possess what is not actually his. Envying one another is used in reference to relationships in Galatians 5:26.

Hating emphasizes detesting and despising someone else. It focuses upon a person's emotions and may include anger, or even rage. The danger in hatred is that it becomes a motive for behavior. It can become a compulsion. Hating one another is used in reference to relationships in Titus 3:3.

These various positive and negative attributes describe some of the concerns of the New Testament church. In counsel and ministry, these became the focus of behavioral and attitudinal objectives. Christian counselors today can also apply these qualities in ministry. These attributes can be goals of positive, godly behavior or ungodly attitudes and traits to avoid.

Suggestions for Application

The principles of Jesus, Paul, and the New Testament church provide examples for contemporary pastoral counseling. The following are suggestions for applying the dynamics discussed in this chapter:

1. Clarify the responsibility of the counselee in

every session. Communicate the counselee's commitment to the solution as well as what part he may have played in the development of the problem.

2. Be aware of the final assessment and judgment of God the Father. Final assessment for issues of godliness is not in the hands of the counselor. Therefore, while judgment is a reality, the counselor is called to care and reconciliation.

3. Identify specific ways in which recovery can be identified for a counselee. Set behavioral and character objectives to be met.

4. Instruct the counselee about negative consequences which may occur if counsel is rejected. Also communicate your commitment to the protection of the counselee, especially for the spiritual struggles that may be occurring.

5. Develop guiding principles for counselees. An example would be "speaking the truth in love." These will give general direction for counselees when they encounter various kinds of situations.

6. Give counselees examples of specific behaviors to follow. These should reflect the principles laid out in counseling.

7. Emphasize the primacy of forgiveness. It is a major catalyst for relating to others and dealing with imperfections.

8. Give specific assignments which implement behaviors discussed. These assignments should reflect the kind of specificity Paul used.

9. Translate behaviors into beliefs and motivations. Behind actions are attitudes.

10. Encourage counselees to pursue both behavioral and attitudinal changes.

11. Develop a vocabulary using biblical terms for behavior and attitude. Use of Bible words helps to focus attention on the work of the Lord in the life of the counselee.

12. Use negative attributes to avoid as well as positive traits to develop. Both are therapeutic and have counseling value. They are in fact necessary.

Chapter 3

THE PASTORAL COUNSELOR AS SHEPHERD, TEACHER AND COMFORTER

In chapter 1 the shepherding motif was mentioned as a paradigm for Christian counselors, and themes identified with shepherding—such as feeding and protecting—were applied to counseling. Shepherding is an effective biblical metaphor with which to temper and guide Christian counseling.

This chapter highlights the shepherding motif from the perspective of Ezekiel 34 and John 10. Insights from these books provide personal and methodological models for Christian counselors today.

The Shepherding Paradigm of Ezekiel 34

Woe to the Shepherds Who Feed Themselves (34:1-3)

The message of Ezekiel 34 is a primary statement of the Old Testament perspective of shepherding. In this passage God referred to the failure of those who had a pastoral function in leading Judah. The emphasis is upon the spiritual care of the people. Applications can be made to Christian counseling because the shepherding function is part of counseling.

In the initial declaration of verse 2, a woe and indictment was spoken against the shepherds. They were guilty of one essential sin—feeding themselves before feeding the sheep. This is exactly the opposite of the call typified later in John 10:11. There the mark of the good shepherd is that he gives his life for the sheep.

The Manner in Which Shepherds Feed Themselves (34:4-10a)

These shepherds had failed by doing the following:

Shepherd	Shepherding Function Neglected
Did not strengthen the diseased	Relief of pain
Did not heal the sick	Ministry of healing
Did not bind up the broken	Repairing dysfunction
Did not bring back those driven away	Restoration/ reconciliation
Did not seek the lost	Evangelism
Ruled with force and cruelty	Compassion

God's Personal Intervention for the Neglected Flock (34:10b)

In this part of verse 10, God makes a powerful declaration: The flock belongs to Him. The shepherds may assume the flock is their possession to treat as they please. Now, especially when the flock has been misused, God clarifies who owns the sheep; they are His own possession.

Christian counselors have a solemn obligation; they

are caretakers of God's special possession. The flock is held in high regard by the Lord. In the New Testament, Christ died for the sheep. In Ezekiel 34, God intervened for the safety of the sheep.

The Work of God to Do What Human Shepherds Neglected to Do (34:11-16)

God powerfully emphasized His personal intervention for the sheep. The words "Behold, I, even I" represent a statement amplified three times. *Behold* called attention to God's pivotal work. The time had come for decisive intervention. The sheep were already in the "mouths" of the self-seeking shepherds. The repetition of *I* stressed that God himself would intervene. There was no other resource for rescue because those whom God had instituted to care for His sheep had failed to do so.

This section assures the flock God will intervene by searching and seeking for reconciliation of those who have been hurt or driven away. *Search* indicates that God's goal is to reconcile these individuals to Himself.

The intensity and fervor by which He does this is the message of the word *seek*. He would continually look for them no matter where they were or what their condition was. God's love for His people is unsearchable and unquenchable.

God would also deliver and protect them from danger. *Deliver* is translated from the Hebrew word *natsal*. It pictures a decisive, almost explosive action, by which someone is pulled or plucked from the very jaws or grasp of an adversary.

The fuller nature of the deliverance is pictured in a series of phrases: "bring them out," "gather them," "feed thee," and "in a good pasture." These phrases describe a process by which God not only delivers but nurtures. This process of discipleship is vital once recovery has begun. A recovering individual must receive "good pasture" and feed on the things of the Lord under the oversight of a shepherd.

Another description of the shepherd's work is to provide rest—"cause them to lie down." During times of rest and recovery the sheep are strengthened. Sheep require times of rest to digest their food. These times are parallel to the necessity of our meditating and gleaning from the Word and fellowship. This function applies to times of rest encouraged in therapy and counsel.

The ministry of Christian counseling according to the shepherding motif also includes healing and nourishment. The sheep are pictured as broken and sick. Every component of a Christian counselor's ministry can have a therapeutic dimension. The brokenness of lives will persist without intervention. God works for the healing of individuals. The Christian counselor must facilitate that work.

Discernment as a Shepherding Function (34:17-22)

An often-neglected aspect of shepherding and Christian counseling is judgment and discretion. God set forth a paradigm of discretion in these verses. The work of God here is to protect the sheep from one another, to prevent the sheep from destroying the pastures which nourish them, and to protect the sheep from outside dangers.

Ezekiel 34 provides important principles for Christian counseling today. Christian counseling is a solemn obligation and must not be done selfishly. God is vitally involved in the therapeutic process of counseling. The Christian counselor must recognize and facilitate God's action.

The Shepherding Paradigm of John 10

The Importance of Spiritual Perception

John 9 set the stage for the shepherding message in John 10. In John 9, a man was healed of blindness. Jesus took this opportunity to point out the spiritual blindness of the Pharisees. They had failed to perceive the work and divinity of Christ. The sheep must be able to discern who their Shepherd is. Spiritual insight was a major issue and goal in Christ's description of the shepherding task.

The True Shepherd (vv. 1-6)

The first aspect Christ described is the genuineness of the shepherd. The shepherd is not false, but true. He is known by his sheep as their very own. The characteristic of authenticity is very important. Christian counselors need to develop a spirit and mind-set of congruency. What pastoral counselors do and who they are must match. They must develop a trusting, truthful relationship with counselees.

The Guarding Shepherd (vv. 7-18)

Jesus illustrated the importance of protection by calling the shepherd the door to the sheepfold. The shepherd lay down at the opening of the sheepfold, thus becoming the actual doorway. This protected the sheep from outside intruders and kept them inside the safety of the compound. The protecting function is a very important one. The Christian counselor must be vitally concerned for the welfare of the counselee.

The motive of the shepherd is also important. Those with ulterior motives are like thieves. They consume the sheep for their own purposes. The true shepherd is committed to giving life to the sheep. The Christian counselor must have the same commitment to the nourishment and well-being of the counselee.

The identifying characteristic of the shepherd is his willingness to give his life for the sheep. This illustrates the depth of his commitment to the task. He is completely involved. There is no divided loyalty detracting from his effectiveness. This same commitment to effectiveness must be present in Christian counseling.

The relationship between the shepherd and sheep is a special one. The feeding and protecting of the sheep depend upon the relationship. The sheep have a profound trust in the shepherd, and the shepherd has a constant commitment to the sheep. The relationship developed between the Christian counselor and the counselee is also very important. Much of the effectiveness of the Christian counselor depends on his ability to develop this relationship.

The true shepherd is not only concerned about the sheep within the fold, but other sheep that may have left the fold—or that may simply not be part of the fold—are also of concern to the shepherd. This applies to the non-Christian who may come to a Christian counselor. Many people mistakenly believe Christian counseling is only for Christians. However, Christian counseling methods can be applied to unbelievers. Even if a person never becomes a Christian during the relationship or if the counselor does not have the opportunity to share the gospel with a person in counseling, Christian therapy is possible. It is vitally important to recognize that as a shepherd the Christian counselor must be concerned about "other sheep" and make himself available to unbelievers.

The shepherd has a special relationship with the heavenly Father. This relationship gives him strength and direction. This same dependency must be in the life and practice of the Christian counselor.

The Flock's Recognition of the True Shepherd (vv. 19-29)

The trusting recognition of the shepherd by the flock is mentioned in the first part of John 10 and in this latter portion as well. The relationship between the sheep and the shepherd is very important. This relationship, especially as it becomes an authentic and trusting one, is foundational for effectiveness in Christian counseling.

The action of God in the midst of the counseling hour is the most important aspect of therapy. Before a therapeutic relationship, methodology, or insight into recovery, the action of God as the Chief Shepherd is the most important aspect of Christian counseling.

Discipling the Followers of Christ: The Teaching Counselor

An important function of Christian counseling is teaching. Many times people who need specific information can be helped through teaching. Other people may need to develop new insights or learn new skills. The approach of the counselor must maintain the centrality of God's work in the midst of the counseling process. Two primary sources for this insight are the Law and the Sermon on the Mount. The principles of these two sections of Scripture help to inform Christian counselors about important priorities.

Application of Teaching in Counseling as Represented in the Law

The Law is organized to emphasize the work of God. The organization is like a pyramid. The top of the pyramid is the Decalogue—the Ten Commandments (Exodus 20). An expansion of the concepts of the Decalogue is found in the covenant section (Exodus 21—23). These concepts are then further expanded in the holiness section (Leviticus 11—27). The Law is essentially repeated in Deuteronomy for emphasis and clarification to a new generation after the wilderness wanderings. This organization begins with God's pivotal act on Mount Sinai when He gave the Ten Commandments. The rest of the Law flows from this initial act.

In the teaching function of counseling, the Christian counselor must maintain a sense of God's prime direction. All action should flow from an awareness and application of God's guidance and teaching.

The emphasis of God's action is found in the preambles of each section of the Law. At the beginning of the Ten Commandments (Exodus 20:1), the covenant (Exodus 20:22; 21:1), the holiness section (Leviticus 11:1, 2), and in Deuteronomy (5:4, 5), God is clarified as the source of the teaching. Christian counselors as teachers must make this same clarification. The information taught or the skill being learned is not merely cognitive. Rather, it comes with the action and guidance of the Lord.

Major Concepts of the Law Emphasize the Work of God

The major concepts of the Law emphasized teaching the things of God. Key terms used in the Law help to provide principles for the use of teaching in therapy.

The word *law* is translated from the Hebrew word *torah*, which means "direction, guide, and teaching." The definition of the word is affected by the context in which it is used. The context in the Old Testament is teaching the things of God. The teachers of the Law did not claim to be teaching mere morality or religion but a vital relationship with God. This same emphasis must be the claim of today's Christian counselor.

The concept of *judgment* emphasizes the discretion of God. A primary cognitive function in the learning process is the ability to decipher, organize, and prioritize information. The term translated "judgment" is the Hebrew word *mishpat*. It emphasizes the ability to judge, set up, and discern. In the Law, all assessments and judgments found their ultimate standard in God. This meant that individuals considered their ability to discern subject to the judgments of God. This same sense of divine standard applies to Christian counseling.

Commandment emphasizes content. Translated from the Hebrew *mitsvah*, it means "to establish a precept." The content of the Law was made up of many commandments. The teachers of the Law understood that this content was not the result of mere human ingenuity. Rather, there was an abiding sense of divine origin. Though it does not preempt information that results from human reason and ability, the Christian counselor teaches information which has been revealed by the Lord. The counselor is not God, but he teaches precepts that find their ultimate origin in relationship with God. The essential precepts used in Christian counseling bear the same divine claim as God's commandments, since they derive from His Word.

Covenant emphasizes relationship. The relationship between God and His people was an important part of teaching the Law. The covenant aspect of teaching was expanded by Christ in the Sermon on the Mount. The relationship between the counselor and counselee is important. Also, the relationship that each has with God is of central importance.

The terms *statutes* and *ordinances* also emphasize content. The Hebrew *choq* is used for both *statutes* and *ordinances*. The Hebrew word literally depicts the cutting of inscriptions as guides and markers. As with His commandments, the origin of these statutes is God.

The Process of Specification

The process of specification, moving from general principles to specific applications, can be seen in the Law. The pyramid of commandment, covenant, and specific applications in the section on holiness and the Book of Deuteronomy are instructive for Christian counseling. The counselor should establish certain precepts (the Ten Commandments), move to the primacy of relationship (the covenant section of the Law), and then make specific applications for the counselee (holiness section and Deuteronomy).

Application of Teaching in Counseling in the Sermon on the Mount (Matthew 5—7)

The Sermon on the Mount mirrors the pyramid of the

Law. The Beatitudes serve as a list of precepts similar to the function of the Ten Commandments. As relationship with God was emphasized in the covenant section, so relationship with the heavenly Father is emphasized in a section following the Beatitudes. Finally, the kinds of applications made in the holiness section and Deuteronomy are made in the sections following the relationship section of the Sermon on the Mount.

The Beatitudes emphasize character qualities. These qualities develop the inner spirituality of an individual. Their development is dependent upon Christ. The following list of qualities should be emphasized in Christian counseling:

Poor in spirit—realizing God's provision
True mourning—open to God to mold the heart
Meekness—yielding one's rights to God
Spiritual hunger—putting God at the center of life
Mercifulness—depending on God as judge
Purity of heart—purity of conscience, relationship, and motive
Peacemaking—restoring and maintaining peace
Willingness to suffer—establishing priorities according to God

In Matthew 5:17-20, the precepts of the Beatitudes are expanded in the context of the relationship with the heavenly Father. The relationship of the individual with the heavenly Father is necessary for the complete application of the precepts Jesus taught. Teaching must move beyond principle to application. Without a relationship with the heavenly Father, that application will be limited, if not impossible. The Christian counselor must emphasize the development of a relationship with God. Without this relationship, the precepts turn into a moralistic code with limited application. Frequently the result will then be distorted attempts to apply the precepts, thus leading to frustration.

The application section of the Sermon on the Mount (5:21—7:23) begins with an emphasis upon the heart (5:21-48). The teachings of God the Father are found first in the hearts of individuals. As God moves in a person's heart, direction and guidance can be found. The various admonishments Jesus made in this section rely upon the work of God within a person's heart. This law and teaching moves from the internal condition of the heart to the external world of actions.

The second section of application (6:1-34) moves from the internal condition of the heart to an emphasis upon God's action. As the heavenly Father, God is working in the midst of the circumstances and relationships which surround an individual. This emphasis brings assurance that an individual is not alone but God is working both within and outside. This assurance should be communicated by the counselor.

The final section of application (7:1-23) emphasizes accountability. The thoughts, actions, and relationships of an individual are ultimately judged by God. This sense of divine standard is a must for the Christian counselor. Without it, the counselor, the counselee, or their relationship becomes the standard.

Being With Those Experiencing Tragedy: The Comforting Counselor

The Importance of Presence in Christian Counseling

Events sometimes occur for which an explanation is not immediately apparent. Sometimes the reason may never be known. Counselees frequently desire an explanation or understanding about these experiences. Christian counselors must be able to respond with their presence and with comfort during these times.

Some experiences are beyond the counselee's comprehension or ability to cope. *Tragedy* is an appropriate term to capture the overwhelming nature of these circumstances. Because people often are not equipped to handle tragedy, their resources become depleted. The Christian counselor must learn to respond to tragedy with a ministry of presence.

The ministry of presence in the midst of tragedy is very important. Though the resources of the counselor as well as those of the counselee have limitations, presence can remain as a constant in Christian counseling methodology. When methods which focus on emotionality, rationality, behavior, and relationships are not enough, presence can be an abiding contribution to the therapeutic process.

The Ministry of God's Comforting Presence (2 Corinthians 1:3-5)

The ministry of comfort is important throughout tragedy and the grief process. In all stages, the Christian counselor should endeavor to show the kind of care mentioned in 2 Corinthians 1:3-5. These verses illustrate how comfort can be applied in each stage of grief. In the initial stage, it is important to care and support someone experiencing denial and trauma. In the middle stage, care and comfort is needed for a person making a heartfelt cry unto God. In the latter stage, the task is to consistently show the individual how to adjust to his loss. In each of these stages, the foundation of ministry is the very presence of God and the ministering presence of the Christian counselor.

Comfort in this passage is *parakaleo*, the same Greek word translated as "exhort" in 1 Peter 5:1. It is a compound construction of two shorter Greek terms—*para*, which means "alongside of," and *kaleo*, which means "to call." The combined meaning is to call someone to your side. The comfort expressed is the kind of comfort that comes by virtue of the presence of another.

Three other Greek terms in the New Testament are translated "comfort." The first is *paregoria* (Colossians 4:11). It emphasizes comfort which soothes or deadens pain.

Another term translated "comfort" is *paramutheomai*, which means comfort that encourages. This kind of comfort seeks to motivate and strengthen. It is found in John, 1 Corinthians, Philippians, and 1 Thessalonians.

A final term translated "comfort" is *tharseo*, which indicates comfort that endeavors to cheer the emotions. It is used in the Gospels and Acts.

The use of *parakaleo* means that a very specific kind of comfort is being communicated. This kind of comfort is the deepest and most meaningful kind of comfort. The other terms emphasize various areas of comfort. Freedom from pain and release for the physical part of persons is the specialty of *paregoria*. The inspiration of the heart and the emotions is the focus of *paramutheomai* and *tharseo*. *Parakaleo* includes these and more. *Parakaleo* is comfort which comes by virtue of the presence of another person.

Presence assures the person on emotional, physical, and spiritual levels. The presence of another, especially the Lord, assures one that he is not alone. This kind of comfort heals the emotional hurt of loneliness caused by a loss. Presence also brings physical confidence in response to danger and peril from neglect. When a person is in the deepest part of the middle stage, little can be explained emotionally or physically. A person has probably given the loss all the thought possible. At this point the presence of the Lord and others can bring the comfort of the Spirit that goes beyond intellect.

In 2 Corinthians 1:3-5, Paul declared that God has all the comfort needed for any trouble. He is the God of all comfort. This is an inclusive declaration meaning that whatever comfort is required, God's presence supplies the comfort needed most. The phrase "all our tribulation" is also inclusive. It means that the comfort of God will meet our deepest need. These broad, sweeping, all–inclusive claims are made by Paul because God's presence does indeed minister to any loss.

The Ministry of the Christian Counselor and the Believer

The ministry of the Christian counselor and other believers is applied in 2 Corinthians 1:4. Paul said the purpose of much of God's comfort toward us is so we may be able to comfort others. Profoundly, the same inclusive kind of statements are made about the possibilities of our ministry of comfort and presence. God equips the pastoral counselor to comfort others no matter what the grief. He uses the comforting process that occurs in the pastoral counselor's own life.

The counselor must be open to God's comfort in his own life and willing to use that as a resource for counseling and caring for others. This is not the same as saying, "I have experienced the same thing." Everyone experiences different kinds of losses. The focus is upon the comfort and presence of the Lord that has been experienced.

The pastoral counselor can use the comfort of presence as a foundation for all stages of ministry in situations of tragedy and grief. Presence is important for the acceptance of someone else's trauma and emotion in the initial stage. Ministry of presence is especially important when a person is going through deep despair in the middle stage. Presence is also important in the latter stage of equipping someone for new adjustment.

God's Strength in the Midst of Grief (2 Corinthians 12:9, 10)

Recovery and renewal of strength is difficult to comprehend in the midst of grief. Because of the depth of some losses, it is difficult to imagine how one can ever return to any level of normal functioning. When a person eventually feels the impact of the loss, it creates weakness, discouragement, and frustration. In the midst of this, it is very difficult to see how recovery is possible. This perception may be true not only of the person going through the grief process but also of those around him.

Recovery in the Lord is always possible, and it often occurs during the individual's weakest moments. This is the power of 2 Corinthians 12:9, 10. Paul did not deny his weakness. He detailed his inability to find relief from the "thorn" that troubled him (vv. 6-8). Paul identified his weakness. However, he also identified the strength that is present in that weakness. The strength of the Lord does not come after the trouble; it comes in the midst of the trouble. The power of the Lord did not come after Paul gained his strength back. It was there when he was at his weakest point.

Seeing the power of the Lord available to strengthen

an individual in the midst of weakness is very important. If a Christian counselor does not see this, he may be looking for strength without seeing a person's pain. The counselor may focus on the elimination of grief and not the experience itself. Recovery is real, but the middle stage of weakness and travail is also real. Paul serves as a model for Christian counseling ministry. Rejoicing is possible in the midst of pain. This is not to ignore the pain, but to perceive the ways in which the Lord is giving strength in the midst of the pain.

Suggestions for Application

The principles of shepherding, teaching, and comforting which apply to Christian counseling must not become mere ivory tower concepts. The following suggestions are made in order to apply them to the practice of Christian counseling:

1. Categorize counseling methodologies under the general categories of feeding and protecting in order to understand them from a shepherding perspective. Further organize them according to the shepherding functions described in Ezekiel 34 and John 10.

2. Develop words and phrases that help communicate your sincerity and honesty as a Christian counselor.

3. Develop approaches that serve both believers and nonbelievers in the counseling hour.

4. Remind counselees about the central importance of God's work in the midst of the counseling process.

5. Develop a strategy of principles, relationship, and application when using teaching as a counseling method.

6. Organize themes and issues for counseling around the same strategy paradigm.

7. Communicate with the counselee the need for all

elements of the strategy. A brochure or information sheet may be used for this purpose.

8. Continually refer to the presence and action of God in the midst of the counseling paradigm proposed above.

9. Record the times and ways God has given you comfort. Use the care that God has given, not necessarily the issues of your grief, as a resource for care and counseling.

10. Develop passage studies about individuals in Scripture who received their greatest strength in the midst of their greatest trial. These studies can serve as counseling tools.

11. Develop a vocabulary of words and phrases that communicate your presence, care, and compassion, such as "Thank you for sharing your pain" or "I would be willing to listen if you would like to share some of your hurt with me."

12. Develop a list of people and resources who can serve as facilitators for individuals going through the latter stage of grief. When people are ready to receive help, it is good to have immediate answers and resources available.

Chapter 4

HISTORY OF CONTEMPORARY PASTORAL COUNSELING

Christian counseling has a rich background in Scripture, as discussed in chapters 1-3. But part of the background of pastoral counseling today is found in its more recent historical development. In this chapter, the history of pastoral counseling in the United States will be discussed and basic trends and influential figures will be highlighted. Analyses reflecting crucial concerns that have evolved from 1900 to the present will be reviewed. Understanding some of these historical roots and resulting concerns can better equip the Christian counselor.

Concerns of Pastoral Counseling Prior to 1900

Prior to 1900 there was a strong concern on the part of ministers and pastors to preserve doctrine and scriptural interpretation. Much of the counseling done by pastors was in the context of the local church. No formal development of a discipline such as Christian counseling existed. Many of the issues and concerns common in the field of Christian counseling today were considered under the headings of ethics or applied theology in the pastorate.

Pastoring was especially marked by caring for others. It was a natural, biblical process for pastors to emphasize care. This emphasis meant attention was given to individuals on a one-on-one basis. This was the temperament of most of the counseling done before 1900 in the church.

Toward 1900 there grew a greater sensitivity for the changing nature of the personal needs of humanity. The nations of the world had become industrialized. Mobility and isolation began to place stress upon structures such as home and community. As these phenomena affected the church, there was an increasing call to address the complexities and changing face of human need.

Beginnings of Modern Pastoral Counseling Parallel With Clinical Pastoral Education

Soon after the turn of the century, a growing concern for ministerial education developed. More and more individuals became convinced that ministers needed ever-increasing levels of preparation and training. Much of this was justified given the complexities of an industrial society. Issues that parishioners brought to the pew were much more complex. The advent of World War I made individuals more aware of issues of tragedy and grief.

Professions in general required more education. Medical and law schools expanded their curricula to meet the demands of society. The minimal requirements for these professions expanded to include more education. As a consequence, parishioners expected more educational training for their ministers.

A number of individuals were involved in the formation of ministerial training and what is known today as Christian counseling. Some of these individuals and their contributions are noted below.

George Albert Coe was professor of religious education at Union Theological Seminary in New York in 1909. He did primary research in psychology, a relatively new field at the time. Coe developed ideas about the need for ministers to pay special attention to a person's individual interests and preferences. He felt the aim of Christian education was to encourage "the growth of the young toward and into mature and efficient devotion to the democracy of God, and happy self-realization therein" (Holifield, p. 225). He reflected a growing trend to address the human condition through the use of other academic disciplines.

Another formative voice was Gaines Dobbins. In the 1920s he was a professor at Southern Baptist Theological Seminary in Louisville, Kentucky. His position was called professor of religious education and church efficiency. He believed that merging sciences such as psychology with theology would benefit the ministry. A special area of interest for Dobbins was the study of personality.

Richard Cabot, a member of a prominent wealthy family, was a professor of medicine at Harvard in the 1920s. He was interested in medical social work. In particular, he felt the need to include psychological studies in the training of medical social workers. Cabot was in dialogue with theologians and pastors. His proposals for training were applied to ministerial preparation as well.

In 1925 Cabot issued a paper called "Plea for a Clinical Year in the Course of Theological Study." The paper called for ministers to be trained in modern techniques of counseling and care, particularly in a hospital setting. He continued to influence ministerial educators in the Boston and New York City areas. The paper he issued and subsequent events have been viewed as the historical beginning of modern-day chaplaincy training (Clinical Pastoral Education) and modern pastoral counseling curricula.

Anton Boisen was a New England clergyman at the time Cabot issued his noted paper on ministerial training. With Cabot's assistance, Boisen began a training program for ministers in Worcester State Hospital. In 1930 Boisen and Cabot helped to start the Council for the Clinical Training of Theological Students. This group marked the early beginnings of other groups that would formalize pastoral counseling and care in institutional settings such as hospitals and counseling centers.

Russell Dicks became the first full-time Protestant chaplain of Massachusetts General Hospital in the 1920s. He developed extensive training programs for the clergy. Much of his development was in conjunction with Richard Cabot. In 1936 Dicks and Cabot published *The Art of Ministering to the Sick*. The book represented many of the concepts that had been developing during the previous decade. They integrated counseling methodologies popular at that time, such as listening and self-realization. Their program and its popularity continued to spread the idea that ministers needed special, formal training in counseling settings to improve their abilities as ministers.

Concerns As the 1930s Approached

Besides the developments in the area of ministerial

training, other developments made the idea of Christian counseling popular. The period after World War I was marked by a surge of interest in psychology. The ideas of Sigmund Freud and Alfred Adler were popular in Europe and growing in influence in the United States. Especially in the field of education, psychological approaches to problems were viewed as a solution for postwar pressures.

One of the pressures of the postwar period was the shift from a blue-collar economy to a white-collar economy. Factories were still a major force in the country. However, the exploding need for clerical support, management staffs, and educational systems brought on unique problems. Social and family pressures were more pronounced. The populace began to question traditional values. The church was under increasing pressure to respond to these concerns.

Along with the postwar era of new management and technology came a strong rise in pragmatic intellectualism. This idea proposed more-informed solutions to problems. Brute strength and muscle as a way of life was challenged. Smarter, more-practical solutions were sought. Ministers had to approach problems with more information and sophistication, similar to the kinds of solutions people found in businesses and successful economies. The church became more businesslike. The ministry of counseling was under pressure from the perspective of parishioners to be more practical and informed.

Still another pressure was the challenging of traditional ideas. It was a period of social reformation. It was a very liberal era. Conservative values were seen as ineffective. Specialization was important. The pastor who was seen as a general practitioner had to become a specialist in counseling. And he had to be prepared to make radical moves if he was to keep pace with the reforms occurring around the world.

The period from 1900 to 1930 was a very challenging one for ministers. Out of this era arose a concern for the special preparation one might need to counsel and care for the sick and hurting of society. This period was the seedbed for the pastoral care and counseling movements that would follow.

Clarifying the Counseling Mission: Pastoral Counseling 1930-1960

This section looks at the trends that continued into the next three decades after 1930. Some of the major influences of this era will be reviewed. The latter part of the chapter will critique these trends and influences and show that some aspects were valuable for pastoral counseling while others raised major concerns.

Continuing Trends From the 1930s: Defining a New Ministry

Richard Cabot and Russell Dicks continued to influence the growing field of pastoral care and counseling training. They believed ethics and the will of an individual were very important and said that ministerial training should facilitate the natural human process of moral development. Listening was emphasized. Providing encouragement and the development of natural human potential were also very important to them.

The influence of Anton Boisen continued to grow, particularly in New York. He believed scientific methods should be used in the study of religious training. In his book, *Exploration of the Inner World* (1936), Boisen said emotional collapse was a chaotic encounter with God which could lead either to a new integration of the personality or to a fall into total disarray. Those influenced by him emphasized psychological and psychoanalytic approaches to pastoral care.

Rollo May was a young pastor in 1939 when he wrote *The Art of Counseling*. The book was based on the theories and methods of Freud, Jung, Kunkel, and Adler. Within a year he published another book, *The Springs of Creative Living*. May studied under Adler in Vienna and at Union Theological Seminary. Though he later emphasized private practice as a therapist, his early audience and sphere of influence was among pastors. His writings helped further launch the growing trend to bring psychotherapy directly into the mainstream of pastoral care and counseling.

Formative Trends From 1940 to 1960: Equipping the Pastor as Counselor

The merger of psychology into pastoral counseling continued to be emphasized during the period from 1940 to 1960. The trend was clinically based among pastors receiving special training in hospitals and other institutions. During this period, the trend focused on training local pastors directly through literature and seminary curricula.

Seward Hiltner was a strong influence during this period. Hiltner was a Presbyterian minister who served on the faculty of the University of Chicago. He was especially interested in social and cultural anthropology. He connected these fields with pastoral counseling. One of his most influential books is simply titled *Pastoral Counseling* (1949). He emphasized the attention, attitude, and intention of the pastor and felt that they greatly influenced the outcome of counseling.

Carroll Wise was professor of pastoral psychology at the Methodist Garrett Biblical Institute in Chicago. It was connected with Northwestern University. A book he wrote that had significant influence at the time is titled *Pastoral Counseling: Its Theory and Practice* (1951). He emphasized a theology of the personality, dynamic psychology, and counseling based on the methods of Carl Rogers.

Wayne Oates was professor of pastoral care and the psychology of religion at Southern Baptist Theological Seminary. One of his most influential books is *The Christian Pastor* (1951). He combined traditional Protestant language with psychological theories regarding roles and behavior. For many people, he was a bridge between psychological methodologies and pastoral applications.

Paul Johnson was professor of psychology at Boston University. He was a strong proponent of the methods of Carl Rogers. In his book, *Psychology of Pastoral Care* (1953), he translated Rogerian methodology into the context of the local pastorate.

Erich Fromm had a very strong influence upon pastors during this period. He had considerable influence upon the work of Seward Hiltner. Fromm was a refugee from Germany, where he had headed the Institute of Social Research at the University of Frankfurt. His work blended sociology and psychology. He developed and wrote on the tension between self-realization and the recognition of one's insecurities.

Self-realization was one of the major concepts that influenced pastoral counseling during this era. Fromm was against authoritarian structures. He felt submission to higher, authoritarian powers limited self-realization. His best-known book of the time was *The Art of Loving* (1956). Fromm argued for the preservation of one's integrity and said that an individual should be devoutly committed to the preservation of individuality by affirming others. This approach and way of counseling emphasized relationships for the sake of self-realization.

Carl Rogers had a strong influence on pastoral counseling during this period. He attended Union Theological Seminary in New York for a time. He later transferred to Columbia University to study education and psychology. He developed a nondirective, client-centered approach to counseling. His best known work at this time was *Client-Centered Therapy* (1951). He taught at Ohio State University, the University of Chicago, and the University of Wisconsin. Although he found increasing difficulty with implementation of his theories in practical, clinical settings, his approach gained enormous popularity. His method was easy to teach and appeared to fit many traditional Christian ideas such as love and community.

An Assessment of the Early Trends of Christian Counseling

Assessment of the early trends of Christian counseling is important. Some aspects of the modern heritage of pastoral counseling are worthy of endorsement. Others pose serious questions.

One area of concern is the role of the church. Much of the effort of modern pastoral counseling has sought to specialize this aspect of pastoral ministry. This trend has sometimes removed the emphasis from the local church. At times, the role of the local church may have even been diminished or made to appear inadequate for training and counseling. Pastoral counseling, even when done in a clinical and/or private counseling setting, must maintain the priority of the local church.

The role of ministry has not always been clearly defined in the modern history of pastoral counseling. Ascribing importance to psychology may have reduced and even blurred concepts of ministry. Is ministry based in emotions? Is it based in self-realization? How does the counselor know when ministry has occurred? The priority of ministry in Christ must be maintained in the midst of counseling.

In reviewing the recent history of pastoral counseling, it is not clear the degree to which psychological insights have affected the development of pastoral counseling. Some aspects such as medical and biological phenomena require special expertise and attention. Benefits are available from studies of areas such as brain functioning and human social issues. However, this integration can reach a degree that blurs or eclipses the pastoral and Christian distinctives of pastoral counseling. The impact of these sciences upon ministry may have brought an unwarranted result—an erosion of ideas and methods such as prayer and Bible study. These and other methods to be discussed in later chapters may have experienced some erosion in the modern development of pastoral counseling.

In assessing the nature, status, and development of

modern pastoral counseling, some important questions may form a standard by which to assess pastoral counseling: How do we know when a certain technique or theory is more Christian than non-Christian? When is a moral decision biblical? By what standard does a Christian counselor measure success? The standards a pastoral counselor sets determines the kind of counseling he does.

God must be at the center of the assessment and development process of pastoral counseling. He is the reason pastoral counseling exists.

Recovering the Shepherding Function: Pastoral Counseling 1960-Present

This section summarizes the trends and influences in pastoral counseling from 1960 to the present. Various individuals and concepts involved in shaping these ideas will be discussed. Significant changes occurred during this period. Attempts to integrate psychology and pastoral methods continued. Also, there was a surge of interest in theological concerns and the pastoral task became more important.

Continued Explosion of Various Methods

Freudian and neo-Freudian techniques continued to grow in the field of pastoral counseling. Freudian approaches emphasized inner conflict. Neo-Freudian approaches used some variation of inner conflict such as rational or spiritual struggle. The basic difference between these approaches and traditional pastoral approaches was resolution. Many of the Freudian and neo-Freudian approaches did not move the counselee to recovery. They merely sought insight as the goal of counseling. By comparison, pastoral approaches in the past had emphasized that recovery was resolved and possible in Christ.

This period saw a strong emphasis upon behavioral approaches. These approaches emphasized the present moment and teaching new behavior. Training was very important. Looking into the past was not a priority, if considered at all. What a person was doing now was the most important consideration. If a person could change his behavior, he could be a changed person. Pure behavioral approaches often denied the traditional pastoral priority upon the condition of the heart.

Self-actualization became popular in the 1960s and 1970s. Self-actualization was the result of the self-realization movement. The goal was to allow the person to solve his own problems. A loving and trusting environment was emphasized in counseling. These would facilitate the counselee's ability to effectively change. These approaches at times relied more on human potential than the intervening work of God as traditionally understood in pastoral ministry.

Transactional analysis was another popular adaptation in the '60s and '70s. It was a neo-Freudian approach which looked at the inner conflict of the individual. This approach taught that there were three forces in competition with one another within an individual: parent, child, and adult. The methods of transactional analysis attempted to make an individual more of an adult. This approach departed from traditional pastoral concepts by reframing spiritual conflict and de-emphasizing the unseen world of spiritual realities.

A strong interest in small groups arose during this era.

The foundation for this emphasis was the self-actualization movement and earlier emphases on self-realization. Human potential was actualized in group process. An individual could not effectively change except in a relational context. While the movement matched many of the long-standing concerns of pastors for Christian community, the peril was to reduce the importance of individual accountability before God.

One of the more recent trends has been family counseling based on the family systems approach of Murray Bowen and others. Bowen used biological concepts from botanical systems in his study of clinically diagnosed schizophrenic families. His observations and counseling methods led to much of the family systems phenomena today. The approach of Bowen and others was a welcome emphasis on the family. Family ministry had been a strong concern of pastors. However, the emphasis on the systemic functioning of the family did not cover all the social and spiritual dynamics which affect families.

Parallel Criticisms Calling for Distinctive Theological Context

In the 1950s a trend began which criticized the overuse of psychology in pastoral counseling. The complaint was that pastoral counseling was losing its theological distinctive. David Roberts, in *Psychotherapy and a Christian View of Man* (1950), called for a synthesis of theology and psychotherapeutic theory. He felt that psychotherapy could not "understand its own task aright except within the framework of a Christian view" of God and humanity (Holifield, p. 325). He argued for the assimilation of psychology and pastoral functions while maintaining the theological distinctive of pastoral counseling.

Albert Outler went a step further in *Psychotherapy and the Christian Message* (1954). He felt that pastors should not only strive to maintain their theological distinctive but that they should be critical of psychology. He argued that theological approaches were more adequate for addressing questions of faith. He felt that while psychological methods could assist pastoral counselors, the essential core of their task was theological. When psychological methods were used, pastors should use theology to critique and guide their use of psychology.

Changing Positions by Founding Fathers

During the '60s and '70s, a number of the founding fathers of the pastoral counseling movement in the '30s, '40s, and '50s began to respond to the need for theological clarification. Among these was Howard Clinebell, who taught pastoral counseling at Claremont School of Theology in Southern California. In 1965 Clinebell was teaching that the client-centered approach of Carl Rogers had "dominated pastoral counseling literature too long" (Holifield, p. 320). Clinebell argued for methods that were more distinctly pastoral in function.

Seward Hiltner was also calling for changes in perception by 1965. He was suggesting that pastoral counseling should press for more judgments about moral issues. The process had become too passive in a quest to move an individual to self-realization.

Carroll Wise was also making adjustments in his position. In the mid-'60s, he was calling for the use of more active judgments about moral issues in pastoral counseling. He argued for the use of pastoral counseling as an enactment of the gospel within the life of an individual.

Wayne Oates was another founding father who was making significant overtures about theological distinctives in pastoral counseling. In the early '60s he criticized pastoral counseling for becoming a speciality in itself. He felt it had become too far removed from the mainstream of identity with pastoral ministry.

New Trends and Theologically Based Approaches

A number of individuals with distinctive pastoral approaches emerged during this period, including Thomas Oden, who supports the maintenance of traditional, classical modes of pastoral care and counseling. Drawing upon the rich heritage of church history, Oden argues for pastoral counseling as it was found in these historical resources. In his book *Pastoral Counsel* (1989), he presented evidence from church history and historical theology that counseling has been a long-standing part of the ministry of the church. Oden not only looks at the theological roots of pastoral counseling but also the historical roots and argues for a "classical pastoral tradition" based on the historical roots of pastoral counseling in the church.

During this period, Jay Adams developed an approach rooted in evangelical theology. He calls it nouthetic counseling. He emphasizes the centrality of dealing with the sin question. Adams says sin in an individual's life is the major issue in counseling and the pastoral counselor's task is to confront a person about his sin.

Two significant volumes were published in the '80s and '90s on the role of the Holy Spirit in counseling. They were *The Holy Spirit in Counseling, Volumes 1 and 2*. The volumes are compilations of articles by different authors on various topics relating to the work of the Holy

Spirit. However, the vast majority of the articles focused on the use of various counseling and psychotherapeutic methods. They view the work of the Holy Spirit as primary in guiding the counselor in the use of these methods. These volumes represented growing concern for the role of the Holy Spirit in counseling. They continued the quest for a theory and method which of itself—not necessarily through adoption of another theory—depended upon God as the center and source of therapy.

Summary of Current Trends

The trends that have developed since 1960 have ushered in continued attempts to merge psychology and pastoral ministry while calling for theological distinctives that maintain the essential foundations of the pastoral task. The issues of church, ministry, the use of Scripture, and the work of God still remain unanswered. Answers that bear distinctive, pastoral identity are still in formation in the field of pastoral counseling. The remainder of this book will propose methods and approaches in this continuing, formative process.

Suggestions for Application

In order to apply the concepts of the history of Christian counseling to the practice of Christian counseling, the following suggestions are made:

1. Conduct your own study into the roots of Christian counseling. An excellent resource is *A History of Pastoral Care in America: From Salvation to Self-Realization*, by E. Brooks Holifield.

2. Communicate some of the heritage of Christian counseling with counselees when appropriate. This can be done through brochures or information sheets.

3. Clarify your particular identity with this heritage, what you agree with and what you may not agree with.

4. Read some of the earliest writings from the first part of this century which helped to shape the modern beginnings of Christian counseling.

5. Review past trends in order to understand their development.

6. Analyze these trends according to the kind of criteria suggested in the latter portion of this chapter.

7. Trace the roots of modern certifying agencies for counseling and chaplaincy in order to understand some of their underlying historical assumptions.

8. Clarify your own assumptions and personal heritage in the task of pastoral counseling. When appropriate, share with other pastoral counselors, or even counselees, your own sense of pastoral counseling heritage.

9. Develop a theology of pastoral counseling in which you list aspects of pastoral ministry that guide the use of counseling methods.

10. Clarify in a brochure or information sheet the theological priorities you maintain in your counseling ministry. These would include the work of the Holy Spirit, the importance of the church, the significance of salvation, and so forth.

11. Develop methods in your counseling that specifically apply the theological priorities you listed. These methods would include prayer, Bible study, worship, and so forth.

12. Identify aspects of your theological position that are distinctively Pentecostal. As a Pentecostal, counselees may ask you specific questions about the nature of the Pentecostal experience and its impact on counseling.

PART II

A
God-Centered
Method of
Pastoral Counseling

Chapter 5

God-Centered Method Of Pastoral Counseling

A God-centered approach to pastoral counseling proposed in this book is called theocentric counseling. In the God-centered approach, God is both the center and the guide for all that is involved in the counseling process. This means though counselees recover through means of awareness, empathy, and others, recovery is centered in God.

Counseling Centered in God

Theocentric means centered on God. Theocentric counseling endeavors to place God in the center of the counselor's life and counsel. It also seeks to place God at the center of the life of the counselee. Consequently, the relationship between the counselor and the counselee is centered on God, which means that the focus and direction of counseling comes from God. Throughout the process of counseling, the presence and power of God is affirmed.

Placing first priority upon the person and presence of

God is the essence of the shepherding task. In Ezekiel 34 and John 10, the summary declaration is that the people may know God. This is the goal of the shepherd of the people of God. The counseling proposed in this book advocates a God-centered approach to counseling.

The pastor and counselor's responsibility is great. Individuals struggle with many needs. Often the first and only person they seek out for counsel is a pastor or pastoral counselor. When these opportunities arise, the counselor and pastor must be ready to respond. The person may not be as willing to seek counsel later, or circumstances may change.

The pastor and counselor's response needs to be one that focuses upon God. While many institutions and helping professionals are dedicated to assisting people, each one in the helping process is committed to certain goals and assumptions. No one else in the community is by design, role, and function so publicly dedicated to the will and action of God in this world as the pastor and pastoral counselor. The express purpose of the pastoral office is to shepherd individuals to a knowledge of God's presence and power.

A number of variables are involved in the pastoral counseling process, but what is the heart or center? Four centers, or focal points, can be assumed in counseling. The first is the counselee. The counselor can assume that the needs and abilities of the client are more important than anything or anyone else in the counseling process. The second possible focal point is the counselor. The counselor and the counselee can assume that the expertise of the counselor and the influence of the counselor on the counselee is the key to recovery. A third option is to assume that the relationship between the counselor and counselee will create conditions that will help the counselee.

The fourth option is to assume that the action and presence of God is at the center of the counseling process. The most important aspect of the counseling process is not the action or needs of the counselee nor the ability of the counselor. Rather, recovery is assessed by, is made possible by, and is guided by the action of God. God does not necessarily condone all the actions or emotions of either the counselor or the counselee. However, God is active in the midst of the process. Though the counselor and the counselee play important roles, those roles are in response to the action of God.

A number of questions are important and necessary to ask in the pastoral counseling process, but what is the first or central question to ask? In client-centered counseling, the first question asked in the counseling relationship is "What are the needs, abilities, and potentials of the client?" In counseling centered on the counselor, the first question asked is "What can I do to help this person?" In counseling centered on the counselor-counselee relationship, the first question is "What conditions in our relationship will help this individual?" But in theocentric counseling the first question to ask in counseling is "What is God doing in this person's life?"

This section will present the essential elements of a God-centered method of counseling. The various parts of the method will be described in more detail in the remainder of this chapter. The God-centered method is as follows (nine parts):

A God-Centered Model of Counseling

1. The counselor perceives and experiences the presence, power, and action of God as central and originating.

2. Identification of various areas:
   • Spirit and primary assumptions
   • Emotions
   • Thinking
   • Behavior
   • Context of things, people, and circumstances
3. Identification of levels of intervention:
   • Prevention and enrichment
   • Meeting needs and correcting problems
   • Crisis intervention
4. Affirmation in all areas listed in item 2 above
5. Monitoring of changes from one level to another in item 3 above
6. Use of the language of the Word of God
7. Confession and testimony at summary moments
8. Devotion in the midst of counseling
9. Affirming the mystery and power of God's action

The various parts of the theocentric method do not have to be done in order, with the exception of the first item listed. The perception of the counselor is very important. The types of questions that are first asked and the kinds of initial assumptions that are made will guide the entire process. These first assumptions and perceptions need to be centered on God.

The other items listed can vary in order and priority. It is important to note that items 1 through 5 must all be done. If they are not all done, God's work in the midst of the counseling process will be missed. The counseling process is incomplete if one of the following is not stressed, monitored, and affirmed—spirit and primary assumptions, emotions, thinking, behavior and context of people, things and/or circumstances. Depending upon the spiritual condition of the person being counseled or the context in which the counseling is being done, items 6 through 9 may or may not may be used immediately. Not all of items 6 through 9 need to be done, but at least some of them need to be done eventually. Items 6 through 9 are primarily verbal, and item 9 may be primarily nonverbal. If they are all excluded, then it will be very difficult to center upon God in the counseling process. The sooner any of items 6 through 9 are done, the more apparent the theocentric process will become.

The Perception of the Counselor (Part 1)

The first step of the God-centered model is important because the perspective of the counselor is important. It is very difficult for the counselee to see God at work in the midst of his problems unless he has the empathy and leadership of the counselor. The counselor does influence the person being counseled. Perhaps the perceptions and assumptions of the counselor will have a greater impact on the person being counseled than any other factor.

A major problem in counseling from a theocentric perspective is consistency. It is easy to talk about being a Christian, even a Spirit-filled believer. The counselor may emphasize this in a central way at the beginning of counseling. However, the temptation is to then move into, adopt, and predominantly use methods that do not maintain a theocentric priority.

The pastoral counselor can develop a theocentric perception by constantly reminding himself of the need for this perspective. It must be included in the counselor's preparation and made a part of every session of counseling. And the pastoral counselor must exercise this discipline in his daily walk with the Lord.

Assumptive/Spirit	
Seeing God's Work as Central and Originating	
Emotion	
Recognize That God Created Emotions and Ministers to Them	
Thinking	
Subject One's Mind to the Will of the Lord in Obedience	
Behavior	
Learn as a Disciple From the Lord	
Context of People, Things, and/or Circumstances	
Recognize That God Is Active in the People and Context of the Counselee	

Theocentric Areas and Goals

Areas of Intervention
(Parts 2 and 4)

The chart on the previous page lists the goal of each area a counselor addresses in theocentric counseling.

Area of Spirit and Primary Assumptions

The area with the most primary influence upon a person is the area of spirit and primary assumptions. This is the most basic way in which a person sees the world. It is the level of character and intuitive insight. Most importantly, this is the level of the spirit where an individual communes with the Lord.

The goal of counseling in this area is to make God the center and origin of the counseling process. He is to be the center by guiding what happens. The will of the Lord is sought for direction and insight. Whatever steps are taken in counseling, the will and action of God is central. He is also the origin of whatever comes out of the counseling process that is good and wholesome. The effectiveness of counseling originates with His love and ability.

Counseling in this area is transformed by the person of God. God himself makes the difference in theocentric counseling. Counseling is dependent upon His very person. God's action is at the center and origin of the process.

Area of Emotions

Emotions are a very important part of the counseling process. People feel very strongly about issues they are facing. These may include deep hurts from the past, bitterness, and other things they find difficult to deal with and share.

The goal of counseling in this area is to recognize that God created emotions and that He ministers to them. The pastoral counselor can provide care which addresses the emotional condition of a person. This does not mean that the counselor condones every action of a person. But recognition of pain and the extension of compassion is necessary. God created us as feeling human beings. Compassion for individuals is a recognition of God's creation.

Counseling in the area of emotions is transformed by the presence of God. The counselor and the counselee respond to God's presence emotionally. Emotional responses to the presence of God form the essential paradigm and standard by which other emotions are formed and guided. Counseling methods which specialize in emotional attention may be used if they are subjected to the action of God's presence. The counselor can use the presence of God as the agent that transforms emotion-based counseling methods. In other words, there may be principles and methods developed from different counseling approaches which may emphasize attention to emotions. The pastoral counselor's use of these is transformed from a theocentric perspective by the presence of God.

Area of Thinking

The ability to think is an important resource for the person being counseled. Events and issues need to be prioritized and set in order. The person needs to understand the issues related to his problems. Logic needs to be applied to the order and arrangement of events that have occurred. Insight and forethought can be applied to past, present, and future events, and problems can be approached with reason and rationality.

The goal of this area is to subject one's mind to the will of the Lord in obedience. The thinking ability of individuals is emphasized in Scripture through concepts such as mind (Isaiah 10:7; 1 Corinthians 14:14-19) and will (Luke 23:25; John 8:44; Romans 7:21; 2 Corinthians 8:11; Ephesians 2:3; Philippians 2). The emphasis is that the believer submit his mind to the will of the Lord (Romans 12:1, 2; Philippians 2:1-11).

Methods of counseling in this area are transformed by the will of the Lord. Various counseling methods emphasize the use of thinking and cognition. These methods can become theocentric if used with the central priority of the will of the Lord for direction and guidance.

Area of Behavior

If a person's behavior is not changed, very little real change can be assured. Good feelings and thoughts remain incomplete without matching behavior. The actions of an individual reveal the condition of the heart (Matthew 12:34). Good intentions need to be carried a step further into actions.

The goal of this area is to learn from the Lord. The concept of disciple emphasizes Christ's teaching of those who believe on Him. His teaching was not centered around intellectual content alone. Christ taught so that fruitful behavior would result in a person's life (John 4:34-38; 15:14-16).

Counseling methods emphasizing behavior can be transformed by the action of God. Not only does the counselee respond by changing behavior, but the center and origin of those changes is the action of God. His action becomes the model and incentive for changed behavior on the part of the counselee.

Area of Context (Things, People, Circumstances)

This area involves the people and things that surround the person being counseled. People are affected by their surroundings. The context of the individual always has an impact on him.

The goal of this area is to recognize that God is active in the people and circumstances around the person receiving counsel. He is speaking to hearts and moving on and through the situations and circumstances surrounding them. This is an affirmation of the incarnate presence of Christ when He walked on earth. He demonstrated His power over the wind and the waves. This represented His control over the things that affect our lives. It is also an affirmation of the work of the Holy Spirit to move upon lives individually and in relationship with others. Finally, it is an affirmation of the sovereign action and control of God over this world.

God came to earth to dwell among us. He continues to abide with us through the presence and power of the Holy Spirit. The incarnation of God at the center and origin transforms the methods used to assist counselees with their boundaries, systems, relationships, and contexts.

Levels of Intervention and Counseling (Parts 3 and 5)

In this area of the counseling process, the pastor is aware of the severity of the person's need. If there is no immediate, pressing need, the person may need counseling on the level of education and information. This is an effort to prevent something more critical from happening. If there is an immediate need brought on by the occurrence of one or more problems, the person needs counsel on a more in-depth level. This would require attention to certain needs and the correction of problems through individual counseling or group participation. Finally, if there is an actual crisis where the individual is seriously threatened by a problem, immediate intervention is needed. Counseling should take the form of decisive action and help to meet problems that are a serious threat to the person.

The Language of the Word of God in Counseling (Part 6)

The pastoral counselor can effectively use terms and definitions in counseling. Certain terms which diagnose a person's condition—such as functionality, family system, or depression—do not necessarily represent anything opposed to a God-centered approach to counseling. However, terms or their usage that do not seek after the action and centrality of God can move the counseling process in other directions or centers.

One assurance of focusing the counseling process upon God is to use the terminology of Scripture at decisive moments. Nonscriptural terms may at decisive moments need to be used as a major part of the process. However, the concepts which form the critical center of the counseling process will have to be transformed into a God-centered perspective in pastoral counseling. Scripture terms by themselves and in conjunction with other terms can facilitate that process. A family may be dysfunctional, but the root problem may be one of transgression. *Dysfunctional* is a term used in certain types of marital counseling, while *transgression* is a description from Scripture. One of the most important reasons for using scriptural terms is that they remind a person about the priority God has for his life. They place the focus on God, not just human ability or insight.

The role of the Word of God in the areas of the Spirit, emotions, thinking, behavior, and context is illustrated in 2 Timothy 3:16, 17. The Word of God is presented as the basis for change in individual lives. *Inspiration* and *doctrine* relate to spiritual direction and priorities. *Reproof* refers to confrontation which affects the emotions and sentiments of the heart. *Correction* calls for logical changes which reshape the will of an individual. *Instruction* addresses the need to learn new behaviors that are consistent with the Word. *Furnished* refers to the practical and effective use of these changes in the circumstances of life.

Confession and Testimony at Summary Moments (Part 7)

When there is a sense of new awareness or accomplishment in the counseling process, it is important to use it as an opportunity to refer to the work of God. Confession is the admission of one's dependence upon God. This may be when a person comes to the Lord in repentance. Or it may be a time to confess in faith one's need of God. Testimony is a declaration that God has been the principal reason for what has been accomplished. The pastoral counselor and the person receiving counsel were involved, but God was the One who made the actual change possible.

Devotion in the Midst of Counseling (Part 8)

Devotional moments in the midst of counseling provide opportunities for spiritual awareness and priorities to be developed. Moments of prayer emphasize that

God is present now and in the future, working in the life of the counselee. Times of praise and worship recognize the power of God and the honor due Him. Without such devotional moments the counseling time might tend to focus upon the accomplishments of the pastor or the counselee.

Affirming the Mystery and Power of God's Action (Part 9)

God's action cannot be fully discerned or understood. There will be a feeling of mystery whenever God works in a life. Mystery means that something is hidden and not fully revealed. The work of God is known through the Scripture, the Spirit, and God's work through creation. However, all is not known about God or the ways in which He works. Examples in pastoral counseling would be the moment at which a runaway decides to come back home or a wayward spouse decides to be faithful. These moments when the most significant changes occur cannot be totally explained as intellect or emotions. They remain part of the mysterious yet wonderful action of God.

A genuine dependence upon the work of God is demonstrated by faithful obedience to the other areas mentioned above. If an individual claims to be faithful but does not obey in the areas mentioned earlier, the level of faith may be in question. James wrote about this principle of faith and works (2:14-18). The pastoral counselor must work at helping a person develop in all the areas of life: spirituality, emotions, thinking, behavior, context of things, people, and circumstances. For example, a person's claim to spiritual maturity may be in question if his love and relationships with others has not increased (John 13:34, 35).

The theocentric method is intended to remind the pastoral counselor and counselee that God is active in the counseling process. The areas listed in the method may individually be developed with the assistance of special methods that emphasize a particular area. For example, certain techniques from family counseling methods may enhance the area of context. The theocentric method emphasizes that the guidance and direction of the use of other methods comes from God. God is maintained as the One who is at the center of the process and the One who gives direction throughout the process.

Suggestions for Application

The need for the pastoral counseling process to be centered on God is very important. Pastoral counseling that places God in the midst of human suffering and pain must not be considered an ivory-tower concept. The following suggestions are made for application:

1. The first question to ask when counseling someone is "What is God doing in the midst of this counseling process?"

2. Next, ask yourself about the spiritual condition, emotions, thinking, behavior, and context (relationships with people and circumstances) of the person you are counseling.

3. Further, ask yourself and the person being counseled which area has the greatest need.

4. Develop ways of communicating your care for the person, especially in the area of emotions, while at

the same time clarifying for yourself and the person being counseled that you do not necessarily condone all that they do.

5. Identify areas in which a person is not translating feelings and intentions into godly behavior.

6. Help the person think through the priority and order of his actions.

7. Allow the Holy Spirit to impress the individual with the importance of the changes.

8. Use devotional moments in the midst of the counseling session to emphasize the presence and power of God.

Chapter 6

PASTORAL COUNSELING METHODS: SPIRTUALITY

Chapters 6-8 amplify areas covered in the theocentric method of counseling introduced in chapter 5. Part 2 of the theocentric method includes five areas of human functioning: assumptive/spirit; emotions; cognition, or thinking; behavior; and context of people, things, and circumstances. This chapter emphasizes counseling methodologies for the assumptive and spirit area. Chapter 7 deals with counseling methodologies to address emotions. Chapter 8 covers counseling methods for the cognitive, behavioral, and contextual areas.

Emphasizing the Assumptive/Spirit Area

The assumptive area is so named because it is the area of primary assumptions. This is the individual's most fundamental way of approaching life. People approach life with a set of assumptions about individuals, life, God, and so forth, that determine the way they function in life.

Some individuals assume that spiritual realities form

the most basic part of life. Some people may believe in the God of the Bible while others may believe in another god or no specific deity. Others may feel that emotions form the essential patterns of life. They react and respond to the power of emotions. Still other people may feel that thinking is the most fundamental property of humanity. For them, thinking through difficulties and problems is the foundation for good living.

Other individuals hold that behavior is the most basic reality. From their perspective, all that is real is what you see and the way you respond to stimuli. Finally, others feel that relationships to people and things around us is the most meaningful pattern of life. Fulfillment is maintaining an effective relationship with others and one's environment.

The position of this book is that Scripture presents a God-centered position in life. This position is developed first in the assumptive area. The primary goal of the assumptive area in pastoral counseling is to see and experience God's work as central and originating. Seeing God's work as central means that throughout the process of counseling and the various changes that may occur, God is the center, measuring line, and guiding factor. Seeing God's work as originating means God is at the source, the beginning, and the ending of the process, giving power and sustenance in the process.

For the unbeliever, the lack of salvation does not mean that nothing can be done or that nothing will be accomplished. On the contrary, God is still moving in that person's life and the counseling process. Even if the person does not become saved during counseling, God is still working in the midst of the individual's need. This does not necessarily mean that God or the counselor is condoning the person's actions.

The counselor's task is to address needs from the perspective of God's care and compassion so that the individual will feel the impact of that ministry and experience change. This is based on the power of God's work. However, if the person does not know Christ as Savior, the most complete degree of change and the fullest potential for recovery will not be achieved.

Verbal and Nonverbal Means of Communicating in the Assumptive Area

Communication in the assumptive area is often nonverbal. The primary assumptions an individual makes are communicated through gestures, expressions, and movements of the body. Spiritual realities do not always translate into words. Much of the reality of this area is very personal and experienced within. Nonverbally, intuitively, things may be sensed in the spiritual, unseen realm of the spirit between God, the counselor, and the counselee.

Many of the means for developing spirituality in the assumptive area can be verbal. These include prayer, praise, songs of worship, and verbal fellowship with a believer.

Transformation of Counseling Methods

Counseling methods go through a process of transformation in the theocentric method. A counselor may use various areas already mentioned in chapter 5. These include emotionally focused methods; methods emphasizing thought; approaches using behavior; and techniques regarding the context of relationships, circumstances, or things. These methods are transformed so that they are shared in a God-centered way. They become acts, deeds, and experiences presented in the name of the Lord. In the transformation process, the essential characteristic which identifies them is their focus on God.

Role of the Assumptive Area

The Spirit moves in the assumptive area by being the center, that is, setting the counseling criteria according to God. God's will, action, and presence become the central core. The counselor strives to submit all that he does under God and appeals to the Lord for guidance. The measurement of effectiveness is God. This process makes God the center of the counseling process.

The Spirit also moves in the assumptive area by origination. This is similar to the statement in Scripture that Christ is the "author and finisher" (Hebrews 12:2). *Author* is translated from the Greek term *archegos*, which means "setting the mold." From start to finish, the pattern of accomplishment is set by God. *Finisher* is translated from the Greek term *teleiotes,* which means "one who orders or arranges." The emphasis is upon setting parameters and goals.

God is the origination of theocentric counseling. He sets the mold, parameters, and arrangement of the counseling. If anything godly occurs in counseling, it is first the result of His action and presence. He set the original goals and process in motion. Any godly accomplishment is the result of His intervention, though humans are involved in the process. However, to maintain a God-centered perspective, the pastoral counselor and the counselee must confess that God was the origination of the process—the beginning—and the guiding presence and ending.

Transformation in the Assumptive Area
Caused by the Person of God

Transformation of the counselor and counselee in the assumptive area is caused by the person of God. The fact of who God is makes transformation in the spirit of the counselor and counselee possible. Whether the counseling process is God-centered does not depend upon the person of the counselor or counselee or what they do or do not do. Spiritual transformation is possible simply because of who God is and His very person.

The counselor and counselee are responsible to respond to the person of God. Without this response, any transformation God may have begun will not be completed. As the Spirit of God moves upon the spirit of the counselor and counselee, they are accountable to yield, follow, submit, and obey. If there is a problem or difficulty in the counseling process, God's Spirit is already present and moving. At that point, progress is possible, but for progress to become fully realized the counselor and counselee must respond.

Cause of Transformation of Other Areas

Transformation in the areas of emotions, thinking, behavior, and context depends upon transformation in the assumptive area. These areas become God-directed when the counselor and counselee yield to the action of God in the assumptive area.

The other areas are directed by assumptions. The claim of theocentric counseling is that the assumptions must begin with a relationship with the Spirit of God. This relationship is deeper than emotions, thinking, behavior, or context. It is a spiritual relationship that determines the assumptions of an individual.

Once transformation in the assumptive area takes place through the person of God, transformation is possible in the other areas. The following is a list of the means by which the other areas are transformed:

Area	Means of Transformation
Assumptive/Spirit	Person of God
Emotions	Presence of God
Cognition/Thinking	Will of God
Behavior	Action of God
Context of People, Things and Circumstances	Creation by God/ Incarnation of God

The process of transformation occurs in the life of the counselor, the counselee, and the counseling methodology being used. A method may be used which emphasizes a certain area because of the need of the counselee. That particular method is transformed when it is used in light of the particular means of transformation mentioned above.

For example, a counselee may have a need for ministry in the area of emotions. The counselor perceives this need. Methods such as positive regard, listening, and genuine congruence may be used to counsel emotions. These methods become God-centered when they are first and centrally used with attention to the presence of God.

Methods of Counseling Emphasizing the Assumptive Area

For the believer, this area is developed through a variety of means. These include prayer, silence, intercession, inviting the Spirit of God to work, manifestations of spiritual gifts, words of exhortation, and laying on of hands.

These can be done individually or during counseling. They all serve to develop this area of a person's life.

Devotions can be used in counseling to foster growth in the assumptive area. Devotion is exercising a sense of accountability to God. It dedicates the counseling to God and is a constant admission before one another that God's goals set the goals for the counseling. This does not ignore the goals of the counselee or the counselor. However, devotion submits these goals to the standards of God and reevaluates them.

Communicate Theology of God's Active Sovereignty

The counselor must communicate a sense that God is actively sovereign; that is, He has not set goals for the process and then departed. Rather, He is dynamically involved in the formation of the individual. He is sovereign in His power, might, and dominion. However, He is active because of His love, mercy, and grace. The counselor can communicate that God is active in His love and in control at the same time. The counselee can respond to God as God, knowing that the Lord will respond to him.

Analysis Regarding Spiritual Maturity

A vital component of theocentric counseling is an assessment of the spiritual maturity of the individual. Besides asking questions about family background, level of thinking ability, condition of emotions, and so forth, the counselor must ask about spiritual condition. Is the individual a Christian? Does he maintain a regular devotional life? Is God a priority, if not the central priority, of his life?

Use Themes Which Integrate the Other Areas With the Assumptive Area

Emotions, thinking, behavior, and context can be connected with the assumptive, spiritual area through biblical themes. Some examples include forgiveness, love, hope, and repentance. These themes depend upon the spiritual level for their life and power. In addition, the other areas must be involved as well. For example, in repentance, emotions are remorseful. Thinking is changed to godly thoughts. Behavior is changed and patterned after Christ. And new relationships are formed in the context of the church. Such integrative themes can become useful in bridging the various applications of the assumptive area.

Sensitivity of Conscience

The assumptive area is especially dictated by conscience, the unseen area of living that is deeper than mere emotions. Conscience connects with the human spirit. The Spirit of the Lord communes directly to the conscience of an individual. The pastoral counselor must be willing and able to appeal to the conscience of an individual. While some of this is nonverbal, words can also address the conscience. Bible words are especially important. The counselor must recognize the direct intervention of God in the conscience.

The term translated "conscience" (*suneidesis*) is formed from two Greek words, *sun* (with) and *eidos* (insight). In combination, they refer to the insight a person has within. The concept is the same as using the assumptions and matters of the spirit within a person to perceive the most essential and primary matters of life. With the conscience an individual is able to give perspective for all of his life.

The perception of the conscience in turn affects all other areas of a person's being, including the areas mentioned under the theocentric method—emotions; thinking/cognition; behavior; and context of people, things, and circumstances. The following chart lists the primary texts used in Scripture to refer to conscience. The theocentric area, the Scripture reference, and the phrase conscience is coupled with are all indicated.

Area Applied	"Conscience" in Scripture	Phrase
Assumptive	John 8:9	"convicted"
Assumptive	Acts 23:1	"before God"
Context—People	Acts 24:16	"void of offence toward God and men
Cognition	Romans 2:15	"hearts . . . thoughts"
Assumptive	Romans 9:1	"witness in the Holy Ghost"
Context—People	Romans 13:5	"be subject"
Behavior	1 Corinthians 8:7	"eat"
Context—People	1 Corinthians 8:12	"brethren . . . wound"
Behavior	1 Corinthians 10:25	"eat"
Context—People	1 Corinthians 10:27	"them that believe not"
Assumptive	2 Corinthians 1:12	"testimony . . . conversation"

Assumptive—People	2 Corinthians 4:2	"dishonesty. . . walking"
Behavior God"	2 Corinthians 4:2	"in the sight of
Assumptive	2 Corinthians 5:11	"Knowing . . . terror of the Lord"
Emotions	1 Timothy 1:5	"charity"
Assumptive	1 Timothy 1:19	"faith"
Assumptive faith"	1 Timothy 3:9	"mystery of the
Behavior/Cognition	1 Timothy 4:2	"lies in hypocrisy . . . seared"
Assumptive	2 Timothy 1:3	"my prayers"
Cognition	Titus 1:15	"pure . . . mind"
Assumptive	Hebrews 9:9	"gifts and sacrifices"
Behavior	Hebrews 9:14	"purge . . . works"
Assumptive	Hebrews 10:2	"purged"
Behavior	Hebrews 10:22	"with true heart"
Context—Things	Hebrews 13:18	"in all things . . live honestly"
Emotions	1 Peter 2:19	"endure grief, suffering"
Context—People	1 Peter 3:16	"good conversation"
Assumptive	1 Peter 3:21	"filth of the flesh"

Clarity About the God of Scripture

The most essential issue of the assumptive area is to clarify that not just any god is being sought in the area of the spirit and assumption. The God revealed in the Bible through Jesus Christ by the work of the Holy Spirit is the essence of the assumptive and spirit area.

The pastoral counselor must not only stress the importance of the assumptive and spirit area but also the God of that area. The center of the theocentric method is not just any spirit but the God revealed in the Bible. Without this emphasis, the theocentric method joins countless other methods such as Jung, Maslow, and transpersonal methodologies of counseling which emphasize the spirit of any number of dieties, the spirit of man, universal spirit, transcendent spirit, and so forth, above God as revealed in Jesus Christ.

This need for clarity makes the Judeo-Christian faith all that more important. The Bible is not merely a document steeped in tradition. Scripture is the result of the inspiration of God. The Word reveals God in Jesus Christ. God also reveals Himself in the context of history. The Bible is the guide and authority for the church. The Holy Spirit in the assumptive/spirit area is the means by which the revelation is applied to lives. Pastoral counselors affirm this reality by using the Bible as the means by which the true God of the Bible is clarified.

The Holy Spirit in Counseling

In the assumptive area, the pastoral counselor must also depend upon the work of the Holy Spirit. The Holy Spirit is the very presence of God. The Holy Spirit brings God himself into the counseling experience.

The pastoral counselor can facilitate the work of the Holy Spirit by being sensitive to the Spirit during counseling. The first step in bearing the presence of the Holy Spirit in counseling is to ask the theocentric question "What is God doing?" This question sets the perception of the counselor upon the Holy Spirit. The next important step is to be open to the leading of the Spirit and willing to follow His direction.

Since the work of the Holy Spirit is unseen and in the assumptive/spirit realm, the counselor must be adept in that area. Counseling in the area of the spirit also includes emotion, cognition, behavior, and context. However, the distinctives of the assumptive/spirit area must be maintained. For example, the operation of the Holy Spirit in the spirit area cannot be completely perceived by cognition. Responses to the Holy Spirit include cognition but are primarily spirit and not subject completely to cognition.

A primary text for the operation of the Holy Spirit in counseling is 1 Corinthians 2 and 3. In that passage, the primacy of the Holy Spirit is emphasized. Two major points are made: (1) The distinctiveness of the Holy Spirit in comparison to emotions, thinking, behavior, and context is clarified. (2) The primacy of the Holy Spirit in comparison to the other areas is stressed. That is, the work of the Holy Spirit is not just another category. His work is the primary agent in effecting change in the human condition.

For the pastoral counselor to be theocentric, he must be open and able to follow the Holy Spirit in his counseling. Being able to follow the Holy Spirit is the key to being one with the work of God in the counseling process. It is important to note that this is not the only task in pastoral counseling. For the work of the Holy

Spirit to be complete, the other areas must be given attention because the Holy Spirit himself is attending to emotions, thinking, behavior, and context at the same time He is moving in the realm of assumption and spirit. If the counselor ignores the Holy Spirit or only addresses the assumptive area, the counseling will not be theocentric or scriptural.

Counseling in the Spirit Realm

In light of the nature of counseling in the assumptive/spirit area, several dynamics described in Scripture apply to the counseling setting. These dynamics have been manifested in various counseling settings but may not have been recognized or admitted to be spiritual in nature. The manifestations of the spirit area are not in a vacuum. They occur in congruence with emotional, cognitive, behavioral, and contextual expressions. However, the realities of the spirit dimension must be addressed for any counseling, especially theocentric counseling.

A key passage describing the dynamics that occur in the spirit realm in the midst of counseling is Ephesians 6:10-21. The following principles can be applied:

Verse	Dynamics
10	Reliance upon God as the center and origin
11	God is the protection against ungodly spirits.
	"Wiles" (strategies) are used by ungodly spirits.
12	"Wrestle" indicates intense engagement and struggle.
	Spirit realities are not from flesh and blood.
	Organization of spirit realities:
	"Principalities"—regions of influence or control

"Powers"—use and appropriation of resources

"Rulers of darkness"—sphere of authority over spirits

"Of this world"—source/center of ungodly spirits

"Spiritual wickedness"—assumptive/spirit area

"High places"—worship and ritual

13   Ability against evil must be theocentric.

14   "Truth" is a means of constant support—cognitive.

"Breastplate of righteousness"— emotional area

15   "Feet shod" applies to manner of living.

16   "Faith"—assumptive/spirit ability against evil

17   "Helmet"— cognitive protection

"Sword"—weapon and standard of Word of God

18   "Prayer"— assumptive/spirit area

19   "Mouth"— declaration and speech—context

20   "Bonds"— context

21   "Beloved brother"—necessity of support—context

Pastoral counsel in the realm of the spirit must not depend upon the counselor to dialogue or maneuver against spirits. The ability of God against spirits is central and the origin of the process.

Suggestions for Application

In order to apply some of the concepts of the assumptive or spiritual dimension the following suggestions are made:

1. In assessing the needs of an individual, develop questions which look at their level of spirituality.

2. Find out which methods work best for you in the assumptive area. Some that have been mentioned

include prayer, direct references to spiritual matters, waiting on the Spirit, moments of devotion, and so forth.

3. Redefine the other areas of pastoral counseling—emotions, thinking, behavior, and context—according to the centrality of the spiritual area.

4. Develop a vocabulary that communicates the centrality and origin of the level of spirit. Such phrases as "I believe the Lord is with us" or "I thank the Lord for what has been accomplished here" could be used.

Chapter 7

PASTORAL COUNSELING METHODS: EMOTIONALITY

In this chapter we will explore the importance of emotions. The pastoral counselor must learn to assess and minister to the emotions of an individual. Some counseling methods have made emotions central to the counseling process. The pastoral counselor must minister to emotions with the central focus upon God. This chapter will look at assessment and counseling the emotional part of individuals, while maintaining a theocentric focus.

Integration With Theocentric Counseling Methodology

The goal of counseling emotions from a theocentric perspective is to recognize that God created emotions and that he ministers to them. God did not label emotions as bad. His creation included the range of emotions individuals experience. This makes life rich and rewarding. It helps an individual respond in a personal and godly way. Emotions can become distorted, however, and lead a person astray. The pastoral counselor must approach emotionality from a God-centered perspective, affirming the godly potential of emotions.

Point of Transformation: The Presence of God

Emotions are response mechanisms. They are the glue of relationships. They are used to respond to others. The presence of God transforms the emotions of an individual. God's presence forms the most basic relationship of an individual's life. When emotions can affirm this relationship and when this relationship can shape emotions, therapy begins to take place in a life. When a person realizes that God is present, he can begin to relate and respond emotionally to God. The emotions in one's relationship with God begin the transformation of the individual's overall emotional condition.

Counseling methods which address emotions are transformed by the presence of God. A counselor may use positive affirmation, reflection of emotions, or any number of counseling methods which address emotions. These methods are transformed by the affirmation of the presence of God. The transformation means that counselor and counselee not only see the emotions themselves, but they also begin to see and experience emotions in a triad of relationships that include the counselor, the counselee, and God. This triad transforms their emotions. God becomes centrally involved with the counselor and counselee in the processing of their emotions.

Assessment of Emotional Needs

In theocentric methodology a counselor must assess all areas of functioning. This was reviewed earlier, in chapter 5, when theocentric methodology was initially described. These areas include spirit, emotions, thinking, behavior, and context. The counselor monitors these areas to see which area needs the most attention. While addressing the area with the greatest need for attention, he also makes sure the other areas are not neglected. Also, when ministering to one area, the other areas are automatically affected. As a result, the pastoral counselor must monitor the impact upon the other areas as well.

When There Is an Emphasis Upon Emotional Needs

At times the pastoral counselor may perceive that attention needs to be given to the area of emotions. A person may be compelled or driven emotionally and in need of regulation of his emotions. An individual may be depressed emotionally and in need of encouragement. The counselor may observe that a counselee is confused about which emotions may be appropriate and therefore in need of guidance. These are some of the basic categories which may draw a counselor to address the emotional needs of a person.

Specific methods for addressing emotionally focused problems will be covered later in discussions concerning stress, burnout, and so forth. The remainder of this particular chapter will deal with the importance of terminology when assessing and counseling in the emotionality area and the impact of dynamics of grief and tragedy upon emotions.

The Importance of Words

When counseling emotional needs, the use of terms is very important. Much of the experience of emotions is nonverbal. The counselor must be able to communicate in the nonverbal area. However, for effective progress, verbal communication of emotions is vital. Words help clarify emotions. Often, the counselee's emotions remain confused and distorted without articulation. The pastoral counselor must develop a vocabulary which effectively deals with the specific emotional problems. One particular resource which provides a system for analyzing emotionally based terms is *The Art of Helping*, by Robert R. Carkhuff. Some of the analyses of terms which follow are an adaptation of Carkhuff's.

Words of happiness. Certain words convey emotions of happiness for an individual. This may be a particular condition in which the person feels relief from pain, a sense of accomplishment, or fulfillment. Happiness may be communicated with varying degrees of intensity. Words that convey a high sense of happiness include *excited, elated,* and *overjoyed.* Words that communicate a more moderate experience of happiness include *cheerful, up,* and *good.* Words that indicate a lesser degree of happiness include *glad, contented,* and *satisfied.*

Analysis of the intensity and presence of happiness as opposed to some other emotion can direct the pastoral counselor. For example, if happiness is present, an individual may be encouraged to continue aspects of happiness or redirect his happiness to other areas or relationships where the emotion of happiness would be helpful.

Words of sadness. Certain words convey emotions of sadness for an individual. A person may have experienced a deep loss or tragedy. There may have been a troubling event that has just taken place. Several things may have bothered someone for quite some time. He may have failed to see the hand of God moving in his life and as a result felt sadness and despair. Words that communicate a deep sense of sadness include *hopeless,* *depressed,* and *devastated.* Words communicating a moderate amount of sadness include *upset, distressed,* and *sorry.* Words that communicate a lower level of sadness include *down, low,* and *bad.*

The pastoral counselor can respond with care when these terms are used by the counselee. Empathy and sensitivity are important. Even though the pastoral counselor may not condone all the actions of the counselee, compassion can still be used in response to sadness.

Words of anger. Certain words convey emotions of anger. A person may be troubled. He may be reacting to someone or a situation. He may have failed to yield a certain part of his life to the Lord, resulting in anger. It is important for a counselor to be aware of anger. Especially important is perceiving the level of anger. Words that convey a deep sense of anger include *furious,* *seething,* and *enraged.* Words communicating a moderate amount of anger include *agitated, frustrated,* and *irritated.* Words communicating a minimal amount of anger may include *uptight, dismayed,* and *annoyed.*

A person may not actually say, "I am angry." It may be difficult to perceive smaller levels of anger. Nevertheless, the pastoral counselor must be able to interpret the presence or absence of anger. If the pastoral counselor fails to properly deal with issues of anger, a person may continue to persist in problem behavior.

Words of fear. Certain words convey the presence of fear. A person may be afraid because of something that has already happened. He could be afraid of something that has not happened but the anticipation has brought on fear. He may be fearful because of a weakness in his relationship with God. Words that convey deeper levels of fear include *fearful, afraid,* and *threatened.* Words communicating a medium amount of fear include *edgy, insecure,* and *uneasy.* Words communicating a minimal amount of fear include *timid, unsure,* and *nervous.*

Various reactions can occur in response to fear. Individuals can become depressed because of fear. Others can become stressed or immobilized. The pastoral counselor can assist in the reversal of these conditions if he can first assess the presence or absence of fear.

Words of confusion. Certain words can indicate that a person may be confused. It may be difficult to sort out conclusions. A person may have difficulty in perceiving the options he may have available. He may not be able to see the will of God for his life. Words that convey a deep sense of confusion include *bewildered, trapped,* and *troubled.* Words communicating a medium amount of confusion include *disorganized, mixed-up,* and *awkward.* Words communicating a minimal amount of confusion include *bothered, uncomfortable,* and *undecided.*

The pastoral counselor can assist the confused person by offering support and clarity. Confusion carries an emotional side which needs comfort and support. It also bears mental agony that needs clarity in thinking. When the pastoral counselor is aware of confusion in the counselee, he can use emotional support as well as assistance with the mental perception of the person.

Words of strength. Certain words can indicate that a person may feel strengthened. This is especially important for two reasons. First, a counselor needs to be able to determine the level of strength in the counselee when counseling first begins. Also, he needs to be able to assess any improvement in the level of strength in the person as counseling continues. Words that convey a high level of strength include *potent, super,* and *powerful.* Words communicating a medium amount of strength include *energetic, confident,* and *capable.* Words indicating a minimum of strength include *sure, secure,* and *solid.*

Words of weakness. Certain words can indicate that a person may feel weak. As with words of strength, it is important to perceive levels of weakness. The counselor must be able to perceive levels of weakness initially and during the counseling process. Emotions of weakness may indicate openness to counseling. However, if an individual is too weak, he may not be able to effectively receive counseling. The counselor may need to work on edifying the counselee before working on more intensive aspects of counseling.

Words that convey deeper levels of weakness include *overwhelmed, impotent,* and *vulnerable.* Medium levels of weakness can be indicated by *incapable, helpless,* and *insecure.* Minimal levels of weakness can be indicated by *shaky, unsure,* or *bored.*

The Place of Emotions in the Process of Loss

Emotions are often displayed when the counselee feels a sense of loss. It may regard something personal—an aspect of relationships or circumstances. A personal loss may be loss of face, reputation, or physical health. Losses in relationship may include death, separation, or abandonment. Circumstantial loss may be financial failure, loss of employment, or an accident. In counseling, it is helpful to understand emotions in the context of these losses.

God created emotions. These emotions assist with the various phases of a loss. Throughout the process of these various emotions, God is present with His comfort and care (2 Corinthians 1:1-5). The pastoral counselor must also minister with compassion and care throughout these various phases.

Pastoral Counseling and the Process of Grief

The purpose of this section is to look at the relationship between the process of grieving and pastoral counseling. A lot of pastoral counseling ministry is done with individuals in great need. Depression, despair, anxiety, crisis, and many other conditions beset people in need of the care of a pastoral counselor. The dynamics of these conditions can be understood many times by looking at the process of grieving. Grieving is an overall response to a number of different kinds of problems. Understanding the grief process can be beneficial for the pastoral counselor as he counsels individuals and families.

General Definition of Grief

Grief can be defined as the loss of anything or anyone meaningful in our lives. Individuals can lose friends, spouse, children, home, job, material comforts, health, money, face, security, or any number of other things or people that have become meaningful to us. People spend a good deal of their lives seeking those things and relationships that they feel will make life meaningful. When any of these are lost, it triggers a sense of grief.

The process of grief is not something that people are bound to experience but something that has consistently occurred in the lives of many. A loss may not necessarily initiate an experience of grief. However, if there is very much meaning attached to the loss, a grief reaction is likely. This does not mean that someone is fated to despair. Grief is part of human experience.

The process of grief and loss described in the rest of the chapter can be illustrated with the diagram on the following page.

Initial Phases of Loss and Grief

During the initial phases of a loss, a variety of emotional response occurs. These include emotions of anger, fear, and denial. Emotions during this phase are nearly impossible to fully understand. It is important to address this period of loss and emotional adjustment with pastoral care. Explanations that appeal to the rationality of an individual would be more appropriate during the latter phases of loss. The initial emotions during loss are intensely negative and very reactive. The pastoral counselor must give effective care for the emotional condition of the counselee.

The counselor should offer support without

The Grief Process

Initial Phase

Loss
Shock
Denial
Physical Reaction
Emotional Release
Anger
Guilt Feelings
Separation From Others/Isolation
Lowered Ability
Inability to Cope

Deepest Part of Grief

Latter Phase

New Abilities
Adjustments
Acceptance
Depression

necessarily using explanations. Explanations are more appropriate for cognitive, thinking, needs. The counselee in the initial phases does not need cognitive counseling, that is, explanations. Rather, he needs counseling which addresses his emotions.

After the onset of the loss, the initial stage is marked by a number of different factors. They may not all occur. However, they are generally all possible. These symptoms include denial, shock, emotional release, physical symptoms, guilt, hostility, resentment, and anger. The next chapter will deal with how to minister to individuals experiencing these symptoms.

A strong indicator of the persistence of this initial stage is denial. Rationalizations, emotional rejection, and wishing away the impact may occur in denial. Denial is frequently part of the grief experience. As long as a person persists in denial, recovery is unlikely. A person may admit to only part of the loss but deny the fuller impact of the experience. The person may say that it is not that bad or it does not really hurt. An individual may say that he has had an immediate recovery. In any case, these are denials of the actual impact of the loss.

Middle Phases of Loss and Grief

The middle phases of loss encompass emotions that result in depression and despair. Emotionally, a person feels very little hope. There is a greater sense of isolation. The weight of the loss is being felt. There may be accompanying confusion or distortion of thought. Rather than just reacting, a person is wrestling with the implications of the loss. The pastoral counselor must continue to minister compassion while giving spiritual guidance. Much of the guidance can provide watchful care. The counselee may be nearer to accepting explanations and insights. However, the need for empathy is still greater.

Entry into the middle stage of grief is marked by increased feelings of isolation and separation from others. Individuals may intentionally separate themselves, or circumstances may put them in isolation. Frequently individuals will feel isolated though they are surrounded by people. However they may arrive at the condition and/or perception of separation from others, it indicates that they are moving toward the middle stage.

In the middle stage those who have experienced a loss will exhibit several other symptoms. A lowered level of efficiency is typical. This does not mean inactivity but a reduction in the amount they are able to produce. They may lose touch with some aspects of what was normal or routine for them before. They may not be able to relate to others or do the same kind of things they were able to do before.

The most critical part of the middle stage is when a person "hits bottom." A person may go back and forth between the initial and middle stages for a time. However, when he reaches a state of deep and constant depression, he has probably entered more fully into the middle stage. This deepest part of the middle stage is marked by the inability to cope with almost anything. The individual feels a very sincere loss of almost any hope. The fuller impact of the loss has finally "hit him."

Latter Phases of Loss and Grief

During the latter phase of a loss a person may have passed the majority of the feelings of despair. God has created a wide range of emotions for dealing with each of the phases of loss. The emotions now are in the form of relief and reconciliation. There is a renewed sense of hope and strength. The pastoral counselor can provide helpful guidance and clarity of thought. The counselor can assist in the pursuit of options.

The latter stages of grief are marked by acceptance and recovery. The person has stopped denying and started accepting the loss. The individual has experienced the deep valley of near loss of hope. There is a renewed sense of hope, but it is coupled with the acceptance that things will not be the same. There is a change. With acceptance of this change brought about by the loss, the individual is able to develop new ways of coping and dealing with life. There is an adjustment to the loss. New abilities are formed to deal with stressors that lie ahead.

In the latter stage the person is not necessarily stronger, but there is an abiding strength that was not there before. It is a new strength. This strength is like new life because it has come out of the death and loss of the past. The new abilities the person has learned are not necessarily "better," but they are new. They have profound meaning because they are what has been retained as a result of the loss. They are valuable because the person needs these new abilities to live now after the loss.

Scriptural References to the Biblical Process of Grief

Grief is not contrary to what the Scripture reveals about human experience. Some have felt that it was contrary to scriptures such as 1 Thessalonians 4:13: "Sorrow [grieve] not, even as others which have no hope." This verse is not an admonition not to grieve. Rather, it merely indicates that you are not to grieve as those who have no hope. The believer, in the midst of his grief, is to maintain his hope of eternal life.

The Scriptures are full of references to grieving and mourning. There are at least 29 different terms for *grief* in the Old Testament. There are many other terms for grief in the New Testament, as well as many references for *mourn* in both Testaments. There is no prohibition against the grieving process. The emphasis of Scripture is that the child of God must depend upon God in the midst of this process.

The terms in the Old Testament translated "grief" and "mourn" include the following:

Words for *Grieve/Grief* in the Old Testament

1. *adab*—whine, high–pitched whine; 1 Samuel 2:33
2. *chuwl*—pain; Esther 4:4
3. *chalah*—weak, feeble; Amos 6:6; Nahum 3:19
4. *charah*—warm, anger; 1 Samuel 15:11
5. *raa*—tremble, fearful; Genesis 21:11, 12; Nehemiah 13:8
6. *kabad*—heavy; Genesis 12:10; 18:20; 41:31; Exodus 8:24
7. *kaas*—turbulence, anger; Job 6:2, grief; Job 5:2, wrath
8. *laah*—weary, disgusted; Job 4:2; Proverbs 26:15
9. *marah*—rebel, bitter; Lamentations 1:20
10. *marats*—sharp, vehemence; 1 Kings 2:8
11. *chata*—miss the mark, sin; Lamentations. 1:8
12. *chamets*—to be sour, great vexation, especially internally; Psalm 73:21
13. *yagah*—to be afflicted with grief and anguish; Jeremiah 45:3; Lamentations 3:32, 33

14. *kaab*—great suffering and grief; Job 2:13; 16:6; Ezekiel 28:24
15. *kaah*—sad or faint-hearted; Daniel 11:30
16. *kara*—to be pained, sorrowful; Daniel 7:15
17. *maal*— trespass which is grievous; Ezekiel 14:13
18. *marar*—to be bitter; Genesis 26:35; 49:23; Ruth 1:13; 1 Samuel 30:6
19. *cuwr*—to turn aside, depart, revolt; Jeremiah 6:28
20. *agam*—to be sad, sorrowful; Job 30:25
21. *amal*—wearisome, labor, trouble, adversity, oppression, injustice; Isaiah 10:1; Habakkuk 1:3
22. *atsab*—to labor, to be in suffering and pain, especially internally; Genesis 6:6; 34:7; 45:5; 1 Samuel 20:3, 34; 2 Samuel 19:2; Proverbs 15:1 (frequently used word)
23. *athaq*—hard things; Psalm 31:18
24. *puwqah*—to cause someone to move back and forth, to stumble, to put an obstacle in someone's way; 1 Samuel 25:31
25. *quwt*—to grow tired of a thing, despise; Psalms 95:10; 119:158; 139:21
26. *quwts*—to grow weary by a thing; Exodus 1:12
27. *qatsar*—to be shortened, to grow impatient and troubled; Judges 10:16
28. *qashah*—to be hard or cruel; 1 Kings 12:4; Isaiah 21:2
29. *ra*—evil; Nehemiah 2:10; Jonah 4:6

Words for *Mourn* in the Old Testament

1. *ebel*—wail, weep; Genesis 27:41
2. *anah*—groan intentionally; Isaiah 19:8
3. *bakah*—weep; Genesis 50:3
4. *caphad*—beat the chest, bereavement; 1 Kings 13:29
5. *ruwd*—wander; Psalm 55:2

The Old Testament uses a wide variety of terms to describe grief. Grief is multifaceted. You may have recognized that some of these terms fit in various stages of the grief process diagramed earlier in this chapter. The range of description is a testimony to God's care for those who grieve.

The New Testament addresses grief and mourning as well. The New Testament uses the Old Testament perspective to interpret grief. There are fewer terms in the New Testament than in the Old Testament to describe grief and mourning. However, the same care and concern as in the Old Testament are still present.

The terms in the New Testament translated "grief" and "mourn" include the following:

Words for *Grief* in the New Testament

1. *lupeo*—sorrow; Mark 10:22; Hebrews 12:11; 1 Peter. 2:19

2. *stenazo*—groan, sigh; Hebrews 13:17

3. *sullupeo*—to grieve with another person; Mark 3:5

4. *diaponeo*—to labor through; Acts 4:2; 16:18

5. *barus*—heavy, oppressive; Acts 20:29; 25:7; 1 John 5:3

Words for *Mourn* in the New Testament

1. *pentheo*—bewail, cry aloud; James 4:9; Revelation 18:8

2. *threneo*—grieve, lament; Matthew 11:17; Luke 7:32

3. *kopto*—to beat the chest in grief; Matthew 24:30

4. *odurmos*—lamentation; Matthew 2:18; 2 Corinthians 7:7

Ministry in the Stages of Grief

Ministry in the Initial Stages

Being aware of the concern Scripture shows for grief, the counselor can minister in special ways to those going through the initial stages of the process. Many of the terms used in Scripture to describe the process emphasize the initial stage. Much of Scripture's description of the human condition focuses on emotion. Many of the terms reviewed above describe emotions. The pastoral counselor can be concerned for and caring toward those experiencing these emotions. He can show acceptance for the person. There may be a wide range of emotions. The pastoral counselor can monitor their reactions, expressing love and concern.

Resistance during the initial stages may indicate a hesitancy to grieve. The person may not accept the loss and may withhold any feelings about the loss. The absence of crying may signal an unhealthy stoicism. Not everyone must cry. However, the persistent blocking of emotions in the midst of crisis can lead to added turmoil and isolation. Individuals may have bargained with God or with themselves, creating a hope that is based on denial of the loss. They may have felt a false sense of mastery when in fact their world was falling apart. The pastoral counselor's sensitivity to the need for release from denial of emotions during the initial stages can help him facilitate the process.

The pastoral counselor can minister through acts of love. Even though the person may be showing forms of denial, the counselor can assure the person of his availability. When the tragedy of the loss does hit him, the love of the pastoral counselor will be a strong incentive to contact him. The counselor can show love by attending to the physical needs of the person. The loss may be so great that a person neglects basic physical needs such as food, health, and proper rest. Being available in love during the initial stages opens the door for further involvement in the middle stages.

The most important part of the middle stage is the point at which the person has nearly lost all hope. It is in this condition that a person comes to realize his strong need for God. He can turn to God in a heartfelt cry or he can attempt to cope through some other means. The "heartfelt cry" of the middle stage will be discussed at length in the latter portion of this chapter. The other means of coping may include ungodly behavior, attitudes, or relationships. Essentially, it represents the continuance of self-centered, rather than God-centered, responses to grief and loss.

Ministry in the Middle Stages

Ministry during the middle stages is very important. This is the time when the person has the greatest potential for beginning recovery. At the same time, this is the most discouraging time for the individual. It is also the time when the greatest dependency upon the work of God is required. However, it is the stage in which a pastoral counselor may feel that there is little he can do. The circumstances and emotions of the grief appear to be the most overwhelming at this stage.

The pastoral counselor should watch for the strength and nature of the person's relationships with other people. The middle stage is begun with increased isolation and separation from others. The pastoral counselor should be aware if the person shows decreased levels of dependency and interaction with others. This may be a form of self-inflicted isolation. In general, the pastoral counselor can be on the alert for any movement a person makes away from others.

As the middle stage becomes more apparent, the pastoral counselor can monitor the individual's own self-perception. He may focus solely upon his own needs. This may be a form of isolation. The person may become apathetic about God. This is further indication of the middle stage. Anger toward God does not necessarily indicate isolation. However, apathy indicates isolation in a greater way. The person may speak of the loss in more personal terms. This may indicate loneliness and isolation. He may perceive the loss as being completely unique and different from anyone else's grief, another potential form of isolation.

Ministry in the Latter Stages

A person moves into the latter stages of the grief process when he has passed through the other two stages. There has been the time of emotional release in the initial stages. The denial of the initial stages has now turned into acceptance. There has been the bottom of grief and the heartfelt cry. The loneliness of the middle stage has turned into rejoicing and renewal of relationships and sometimes new relationships as well.

The person may have touched upon the latter stages to some extent earlier in the process and was able to accept some of what was happening. There was a sense of some measure of adjustment. However, the individual had not come fully through the other two stages. As a result, the person moved back and forth. However, once the other two stages have been more fully experienced, the person is now ready to more fully enter into the latter stages.

Ministry during the latter stages seeks to equip the person with new ways of coping. The tragedy of the loss took away some of the things that may have worked for the person in the past. However, relationships, habits, and attitudes have changed since the loss Thus, it is a time of adjustment. Ministry is equipping the person for the adjustment. It may involve new relationships, a new job, and new surroundings.

The individual also needs to know how to look upon the past loss and grief. The grief of the past is not forgotten. However, it is transformed. What once loomed as insurmountable tragedy has now become testimony and witness. The person is able to remember the sustainment of God and those around him. There is pain while remembering. Nevertheless there is a realization that the person is on the other side of the initial and middle stages. There is a confidence that God has made recovery possible.

Three critical areas constitute much of ministry during this stage. First, the pastoral counselor can assist the person in developing a new network of supportive relationships. Others can be brought into the process to give prayerful support. Second, the pastoral counselor can teach, train, show, and model ways to adjust. These can include new skills, new habits, and new ways to work. Finally, the pastoral counselor can offer the new perspective of testimony and insight. Instead of constantly being despondent, the individual learns new ways to feel and respond.

The Ministry of God's Comforting Presence (2 Corinthians 1:3-5)

> Blessed be God, even the Father of our Lord Jesus Christ, the Father of mercies, and the God of all comfort; who comforteth us in all our tribulation, that we may be able to comfort them which are in any trouble, by the comfort wherewith we ourselves are comforted of God. For as the sufferings of Christ abound in us, so our consolation also aboundeth by Christ (2 Corinthians 1:3-5).

The ministry of comfort is important throughout the grief process. In all stages, the pastoral counselor should endeavor to show the kind of care mentioned in 2 Corinthians 1:3-5. In the initial stages it is important to care and support someone experiencing denial and trauma. In the middle stages care and comfort are needed for someone making a heartfelt cry to God. In the latter stages the task is to consistently show a person how to make new adjustments to his loss. In each of these, a foundation of ministry is the very presence of God and the pastoral counselor. Second Corinthians 1:3-5 illustrates how comfort can be applied in each stage.

The term *comfort* in this passage is the same term as exhort found in 1 Peter 5:1. The Greek term is *parakaleo*, a compound construction of two shorter Greek terms—*para* and *kaleo*. The former means "alongside." The latter means "to call." The combined meaning is to call someone to your side. The comfort expressed is the kind of comfort that comes by virtue of the presence of another.

There are three other Greek terms used elsewhere in the New Testament which are also translated "comfort." The first is *paregoria*. It emphasizes comfort which soothes or deadens pain. This term was used in Colossians 4:11. Another term translated "comfort" is *paramutheomai*. It means comfort that encourages and is used in John, 1 Corinthians, Philippians, and 1 Thessalonians. This kind of comfort seeks to motivate and strengthen another. A final term translated "comfort" is *tharseo*. It is used in the Gospels and the Book of Acts. It indicates comfort that endeavors to cheer the emotions of and to give courage to someone else.

The use of *parakaleo* means that a very specific kind of comfort is being communicated. It is the deepest and most meaningful kind of comfort. The other terms emphasize various areas of comfort. Freedom from pain and release for the physical part of individuals is the specialty of *paregoria*. The inspiration of the heart and the emotions is the focus of *paramutheomai* and *tharseo*. *Parakaleo* includes these and more. The presence of a person brings comfort that includes physical, emotional, and other aspects of a person's grief. It includes the complete grief experience of the person.

Presence assures the person on emotional, physical, and spiritual levels. The presence of another, especially the Lord, assures a person that he is not alone. This kind of comfort heals emotional hurts brought on by the loneliness of a loss. Presence also brings physical confidence in response to danger and peril from neglect. When a person is in the deepest part of the middle stage, very little can be explained emotionally or physically. A person has probably given all the thought he can to the loss. At this point the presence of the Lord and others can bring a comfort of the Spirit that goes beyond intellect.

In 2 Corinthians 1:3-5 Paul declared that God has all the comfort needed for any trouble. He is the God of all comfort. This is an inclusive declaration meaning that whatever comfort is required, God's presence supplies the comfort that is needed most. The phrase "in all our tribulation" is also inclusive. It means that the comfort of God meets the deepest need of any kind. These broad-sweeping, all-inclusive claims were made by Paul because God's presence does indeed minister to any loss. It is the key to all the stages of grief.

The ministry of the pastoral counselor and other believers is applied in verse 4. Paul said the purpose of much of God's comfort toward us is that we may be able in turn to comfort others. Profoundly, the same kind of inclusive statements are made about the possibilities of our ministry of comfort and presence. God equips the pastor to comfort others no matter what the grief. He uses the comforting process that occurs in the pastoral counselor's own life.

The pastoral counselor must be open to God's comfort in his own life and willing to use that as a resource for counseling and caring for others. This is not the same as saying, "I have experienced the same thing." This kind of statement focuses upon the content of a loss. Everyone experiences different kinds of losses. The focus is upon the comfort and presence of the Lord. The experience of the presence of God to comfort someone can be universally applied.

The pastoral counselor can use the comfort of presence as a foundation for all stages of grief ministry. Presence is important for the acceptance of someone else's trauma and emotion in the initial stages. Ministry of presence is especially important when a person is going through deep despair in the middle stages. Presence is also important in the latter stage of equipping someone for new adjustment.

God's Strength in the Midst of Grief (2 Corinthians 12:9, 10)

> And he said unto me, My grace is sufficient for thee: for my strength is made perfect in weakness. Most gladly therefore will I rather glory in my infirmities, that the power of Christ may rest upon me. Therefore I take pleasure in infirmities, in reproaches, in necessities, in persecutions, in distresses for Christ's sake: for when I am weak, then am I strong (2 Corinthians 12:9, 10).

Recovery and renewal of strength is hard to see in the midst of grief. It is hard to imagine how one can ever return to any level of functioning because of the depth of some losses. That perception becomes even more critical in light of the nature of the grief process. A person will eventually feel the impact of the loss, creating weakness, discouragement, and frustration. In the midst of this, it is very difficult to see how recovery is possible. Not only does the person going through the grief process perceive this to be true, but those around him may also fail to see any hope for recovery.

Recovery in the Lord is always possible, and it takes place right in the midst of the weakest moments for the individual. This is the power of 2 Corinthians 12:9, 10. Paul did not deny his weakness. He had just detailed his inability to find relief from the "thorn" that had been troubling him (vv. 6-8). Paul identified his weakness. However, he also identified the strength that was present in that weakness. The strength of the Lord does not come after the trouble; it comes in the midst of the trouble. The power of the Lord did not come after Paul gained his strength back. It was there when he was at his weakest point.

Seeing the power of the Lord available to strengthen someone in the midst of weakness is very important. If a pastoral counselor does not see this, he may be looking for strength without seeing a person's pain. The church may focus upon the elimination of grief and not the experience itself. Recovery is real, but the middle stages of weakness and travail are also real. Paul serves as a model for pastoral counseling ministry. Rejoicing is possible in the midst of pain. This is not to ignore the pain but to perceive the ways in which the Lord is giving strength in the midst of the pain.

A Biblical Paradigm for Counseling Those in Grief and Tragedy: Psalm 107

The purpose of this section is to analyze the work of God in the midst of grief and crisis by using Psalm 107 as a model. This psalm provides insight into the process of grieving. The psalm discusses five themes which mirror the various stages of the grief process. The work of God is illustrated in the psalm. Throughout the various symptoms and experiences of loss, God is active in the lives of those suffering. Not only is the sense of loss real in the psalm, but the celebration of victory is also real. An illustration of the dynamics of Psalm 107 being reflected in the grief process can be seen on page 158.

God's Goodness Active in the Midst of Crisis

Psalm 107 begins with a declaration of God's response to man in the midst of tragedy (v. 1). The response is affirmed throughout the various stages of grief (vv. 2, 8, 15, 21, 30-32, 42-43). The declaration affirms three aspects of God's character and care. These provide a way to understand the work of God in the midst of crises. The first aspect is that of God's goodness. The term for

The Grief Process in Psalm 107

Initial Phase   GOD   Latter Phase

CARE/
SUPPORT
vv. 33-42
Initial-Middle-
Latter

INNOCENCE/
RESCUE
vs. 23-32
Initial-Middle-
Latter

GOOD-*towb* (complete)
MERCY-*checed* (faithful)
EVERLASTING-*olam* (hidden places)
vv. 1, 2, 8, 15, 21, 30-32, 42-43

Heartfelt Cry

ENEMY
vv. 2-9
Initial-Middle-
Latter

BONDAGE
vv. 10-16
Initial-Middle-
Latter

"good" is the Hebrew word *towb*. The term emphasized uprightness and completeness. The goodness of God was the assurance that God was working in the midst of all things for the purposes of His completeness and uprightness. This was not the guarantee of the absence of conflict. Rather, it was the guarantee that God was working for the complete recovery and wholesome renewal of the individual.

The second aspect emphasized in verse 1 is that of God's mercy, which is the Hebrew word *checed* and is usually translated "lovingkindness." This is the translation of the term in verse 43. This love and mercy did not emphasize emotions. The term highlighted faithful relationship. It was love that was demonstrated by faithfulness. The declaration was that in the midst of the loss, God would not leave or forsake an individual. He would be faithful in His love and presence.

The final aspect emphasized is the fact that God's action is everlasting. This term *for ever*, the Hebrew word *olam,* literally means "to hide." The idea of "hidden" applies to the aspect of time. Time is hidden and unknown to a person. Therefore, the declaration is that God is God in the hidden future. The emphasis of the term is that God is the God of all hidden places. This would include the hidden past and present. It would include the hidden places of the heart and human experience.

Throughout ministry in the process of crisis and grief, these affirmations can be made. The psalmist intentionally repeated the call to see these affirmations about God. This is important for counseling ministry. It may be difficult to see these aspects of God's care in the midst of weakness and tragedy. However, this may be the most important emphasis of the psalm. This theme will be mentioned later.

Various Stages of Grief Reflected

Psalm 107 has five major sections. Each section contains a theme (e.g., *enemies*) which identifies with a particular place in the overall grief process (*enemies* represents the initial stage) and the process of grief in miniature within its section (i.e., all three stages of grief—initial, middle, and latter—are in each section).

1. The "Enemy" of Loss

This section covers verses 2-9 and bears the theme *enemies*. It can be identified with the initial experience of loss because loss comes like an enemy. It is unwanted and unwelcome. It is an intruder that takes its toll. It spoils a life and a relationship. The theme is taken from the phrase "the hand of the enemy" (v. 2).

The initial stages of grief are depicted by the words *wandered* and *solitary* (v. 4). The transition into isolation and the middle stage is seen in the statement "They found no city to dwell in" (v. 4). The middle stage is more fully described in the statement "Hungry and thirsty, their soul fainted in them" (v. 5). It illustrates the depths of loneliness and need.

Verse 6 describes the heartfelt cry that rises unto the Lord in the midst of the deepest part of the grief. This heartfelt cry becomes the critical point at which recovery begins. The transition from the depths of the process toward recovery begins with this heartfelt cry. This is one of the most consistent aspects of the psalm. Each of the first four subsections will describe the middle section of the crisis process (vv. 6, 13, 19, 28). In each section the heartfelt cry is described.

The heartfelt cry is the key to godly and full recovery.

It is described in the text as occurring in the midst of, not after, the deepest part of the experience. The text reads, "Then they cried unto the Lord in their trouble." The heartfelt cry is not just a moment of emotional release or catharsis. It is a moment of faith. The grace and mercy of God is experienced. The person cries out, uninhibited by rationalizations or self-centered attempts at recovery. It is a moment of complete dependence upon God. For some it may be salvation. For others, it may be a return to God. For still others it may be an experience of Christian growth. The cry cannot be reproduced through human methodology. It is a moment made possible only by the Spirit of God and the obedient response of the person in crisis.

After the heartfelt cry, the text describes the latter stage. The description is one of recovery and new adjustments. The following describe the dynamics of the latter stage: "He delivered them out of their distresses" (v. 6); "He led them forth by the right way . . . to a city of habitation" (v. 7); "He satisfieth the longing soul, and filleth the hungry soul with goodness" (v. 9).

The psalm calls the reader to remember the work of God in the midst of grief (v. 8). This call is repeated at the end of each subsection (vv. 8-9, 15-16, 21-22, 31-32, and 42-43). Praise affirms the action of God in the midst of grief and crisis. It perceives the three attributes of God mentioned in verse 1. The recognition and praise of God is possible at any part of crisis. The praise does not deny the grief; rather, it recognizes God's work in the midst of the experience.

2. The Bondage of Isolation

The second section highlights the theme of isolation

and bondage. This theme is indicative of the initial stage, especially as it moves toward loneliness and the middle stage. This section is found in verses 10-16. The idea of bondage is stated in verse 10: "bound in affliction and iron."

The various stages of the grief process are represented in the section. The initial stages of grief are represented in the phrases "sit in darkness," "in the shadow of death," and "bound in affliction and iron" (v. 10). The middle stage is represented with these words: "brought down their heart with labour," "fell down," and "there was none to help" (v. 12). The latter stage is found in verses 13, 14, and 16 in the following phrases: "out of their distresses," "out of darkness and the shadow of death," and "brake their bands in sunder," The heartfelt cry is in verse 13. The exhortation to praise the work of God in the midst of grief is in verse 15.

Critical issues that appear throughout all five sections are rebellion and innocence. Sometimes grief is the result of rebellion and transgression. This is the case in the sections on bondage and hopelessness. At other times grief comes upon those who are innocent. This is the case in the sections on enemies and the innocent. The final section on the abiding care and support of God emphasizes God's sovereign action in response to the finiteness of man. This will be discussed under that section.

3. The Hopelessness of Despair

The third section highlights the theme of hopelessness and despair. This theme is indicative of the depths of the middle stage. There is a fuller sense of frustration and tragedy at this point. This section is found in verses 17-

22. The idea of hopelessness is stated in verse 18: "They draw near unto the gates of death."

The various stages of the grief process are represented in the section. The initial stages of grief are represented in these words: "afflicted" (v. 17) and "soul abhorreth all manner of meat" (v. 18). The middle stage is represented in these words: "They draw near unto the gates of death" (v. 18). The latter stage is found in verses 19 and 20: "He saveth them out of their distresses. He sent his word, and healed them, and delivered them from their destructions." The heartfelt cry is in verse 19. The exhortation to praise the work of God in the midst of grief is in verse 21.

4. The Rescue of the Innocent

The fourth section highlights the theme of rescuing the innocent. This theme is indicative of the passage from the middle stage to the latter stage. This section is found in verses 23-32. The idea of the innocent is stated in verse 23. Those in distress often find themselves in "great [and perilous] waters" because it is their "business" to be there. They do not ask to be there. It is a necessity. They are innocent of rebellion or transgression. It is their vocation. This could apply to marital relationships, parent-child relationships, vocation, and many other situations.

The various stages of the grief process are represented in the section. The initial stage and the circumstances that bring the grief are described in verses 23-26a. These verses describe perilous waters and a storm that arises. The middle stage is represented in verses 26b and 27. The description of the middle section is threefold. First, inner turmoil is described: "Their soul is melted."

Second, physical distress is described: "They reel to and fro, and stagger like a drunken man." Third, mental anguish is described: "They are . . . at their wit's end." The description of the latter stage is in verses 28-30. They describe God's bringing them safely to a desired place of haven. The heartfelt cry is in verse 28. The exhortation to praise the work of God in the midst of grief is in verses 31 and 32.

A critical issue concerns God's work in starting the storm (v. 25). There is no explanation. God is not defended. The section describes God's control and sovereign action over the storm. Sometimes the event which begins a crisis or the grief process begins with God. It may or may not be due to rebellion. Nevertheless, God is still sovereign. This is the major emphasis of the last section, God's loving sovereignty.

5. The Abiding Care and Support of God

The last section is a broad look at the work of God in the midst of grief and crisis (vv. 33-34). The work of God in the midst of blessing or tragedy is described. The initial, middle, and latter stages of the grief cycle are seen through rivers and waters turning to a wilderness and then prospering once again. Fields and livestock become barren and then are made bountiful again. Whether God is working to multiply greatly (v. 38) or to bring low (v. 39), He is still the same loving God declared throughout the psalm.

The Importance of Seeing God's Work in the Midst of Grief

The concluding theme of the psalm is the necessity and reward of seeing God work in the midst of grief and crisis. God has constantly been praised throughout the psalm for His work (vv. 8-9, 15-16, 21-22, 31-32, and 42-43). Verses 42 and 43 exhort the reader to constantly see God's loving care at work. The conditions of grief have been graphically described throughout the psalm. But the reader is continually exhorted to keep seeing God's care in the midst of the tragedy as well as the triumph. When a person perceives this, there is a great blessing. The blessing is that "iniquity shall stop her mouth" (v. 42) and the "lovingkindness of the Lord" will be understood (v. 43). The reward is that the antagonism of grief will stop and the love of God will be experienced, no matter what the experience of grief may be.

Suggestions for Application

The following are suggestions for pastoral counseling of emotions:

1. Assess the kind of loss a person may be experiencing.

2. Determine whether a person is in the initial, middle, or latter phases of a loss.

3. Monitor the words a person uses to determine the kind and intensity of emotions.

4. Use the words used by the counselee to describe his emotions. This will keep your focus accurate. Using your own words for the counselee's emotions may carry a different meaning and refer to a different emotion.

5. Assess significant losses experienced by the counselee. Keep dates of events surrounding the loss in order to monitor any grief process that the person might be going through.

6. Use biblical illustrations and principles (to be presented in later chapters). They will give insight for those experiencing grief.

7. Have a list of community agencies that you can contact immediately in order to help someone grieving.

8. Emphasize openness and availability so that those who may feel isolated and are experiencing the critical middle stages of grief will feel comfortable in receiving counsel from you.

9. Present the descriptions of grief and mourning in Scripture to the counselee.

10. Review times when you may have grieved and experienced the various symptoms listed. This can be a resource in ministering to others.

11. If a person is in the initial stages of grief, time is of the essence. Try to implement loving counsel and care as soon as possible. Place a priority upon ministry to those you feel are in the initial stages.

12. Record the times and ways God has given you comfort. Use the care that God has given, not necessarily the issues of your grief, as a resource for care and counseling.

13. Develop passage studies about individuals in Scripture who received their greatest strength in the midst of their greatest trial. These studies can serve as counseling tools.

14. Develop a vocabulary of words and phrases that communicate your presence, care, and compassion, such as "Thank you for sharing your pain" or "I would be willing to listen if you would like to share some of your hurt with me."

15. Develop a list of persons and resources who can serve as facilitators for individuals going through the latter stages of grief. When people are ready to receive help, it is good to have immediate answers and resources available.

16. List the various kinds of griefs and crises counselees have experienced within the last 12 months.

Design specific ways that these experiences may have fit into the cycle of Psalm 107. Develop a way of seeing the hand of God moving in the midst of these events. This does not mean that God condones the actions but that God is still working in the midst of them. Communicate these insights with those who may be experiencing grief or criss currently. Keep the content of experiences confidential, but share the ways in which God has communicated His loving care.

17 Develop ways to foster the heartfelt-cry experience. Some may include sharing the principles of Psalm 107, inviting individuals to admit their sense of dependence on God or to confess that they are in the middle stages of the grieveing process.

18. Develop certain worship themes in counseling which emphasize God's sustaining care in the midst of grief. These themes should affirm that God provides strength in the midst of weakness, not just an escape from the crisis.

Chapter 8

PASTORAL COUNSELING METHODS: THINKING, BEHAVIOR, AND CONTEXT

The previous chapters have looked at the theocentric grid. Each area of the grid has various goals. The emphasis of one area does not exclude another area's importance.

The goals of the cognitive and behavioral areas were stated in chapter 5. The goal of the cognitive area is to subject one's mind to the will of the Lord. The goal of the behavioral area is to learn from the Lord as a disciple.

In each area, a particular aspect of God transforms the methods used toward a theocentric focus. In the cognitive area, the will of God gives central guidance. In the behavioral area, the acts of God lead the person in behavioral change.

Discipleship and Emphasizing Cognition in Theocentric Counseling

Common Language

Relating to the counselee through language is very important. Language represents the thought processes of the person. If the pastoral counselor uses words and phrases with meanings that are the same or very similar to those of the counselee, he will gain insight into the counselee's thinking. With this insight the pastoral counselor can more effectively approach the cognitive needs of the counselee.

Moving Beyond Feelings

Words and thinking help the counselee to move beyond his feelings toward behavior. Focusing upon cognition naturally begins this movement. The suggestions that follow are especially for the counselee who is very emotional but not making progress. They are also for those who function best when they are able to put more thought into an action.

Meanings and Implications

An initial step in moving toward thinking is to identify the particular experience and feelings of the person. This is done by using the basic who, what, why, where, when, and how questions. These questions cause the counselee to think about the experience.

After establishing a description of the experience, it is helpful to reflect on the implications of the experience. This is a critical juncture in moving from emotions to behavior through the process of thinking. It is at this point that misconceptions can occur. Some common misconceptions about experiences include the following:

1. All or nothing—being either a winner or a loser
2. Overgeneralizing—applying one thing to everything

3. Mental filter—one negative detail affects all perspective

4. Disqualifying the positive—rejecting anything positive to maintain a negative assumption not grounded in fact or biased by your perspective

5. Jumping to conclusions—forecasting results before you even start

6. Magnification or minimization—seeing a catastrophe or reducing something to nothingness

7. Thinking with your emotions—not really thinking, just reacting based only on emotions

8. "Should" statements—misusing authority to produce pressure or guilt on yourself or others

9. Labeling and mislabeling—trivializing things or people by prejudicially labeling them

10. Personalization—always interpreting events or relationships in a personal way, easily offended or highly reactionary

Focusing on Difficulties

Focusing on difficulties means seeing problems as they really are. This approach works on tearing down the negative assumptions listed earlier. Problems and roadblocks to effectiveness are not ignored. Rather, they are clarified for what they really are.

Application of difficulties involves clarification of proper responsibility for difficulties. The counselee may not be responsible for certain difficulties and may not be able to change them. But the counselee needs to assume responsibility for difficulties he caused and can change.

Focus on Abilities

Abilities need to be identified and categorized. This is a process of finding out what the counselee can do in response to a problem. The thinking process is further enhanced by assessing the strengths and weaknesses of these abilities. Gradually the counselee begins to see how at least some abilities to change can be applied to a particular problem.

The application of abilities means considering what can be done about a particular problem. The abilities mentioned earlier are personalized by the counselee. He sees that he is actually able to overcome the problem. This is not merely an emotional confidence. Rather, it is the formulation of specific responses to a problem.

Formulate Goals (Time, Routine, Accountability)

In formulating goals for overcoming a problem, three aspects are important: time, routine, and accountability. The pastoral counselor must specify a time in which the counselee will apply the solutions discussed. Further, a daily routine for approaching the problem should be set up. Finally, a method of accountability wherein the counselee reports to the counselor must be set up.

Behavioral Emphases in Theocentric Counseling

This section emphasizes the impact of behavior upon the pastoral counseling process. The goal of this area is to learn as a disciple from the Lord. Much of our behavior is learned in response to the behavioral modeling and teaching of others. Also, we learn in response to stimuli and the results of our behavior. From a theocentric perspective, the counselee's goal is to learn as a disciple from the Lord, thereby learning appropriate and effective behaviors.

The aspect of God which transforms the use of behavioral methods in counseling is the action of God. The counselee's actions are formed in response to the action of God. A counselor may use behavioral methods emphasizing learned behaviors. Theocentric perspective transforms these methods by including focus upon the action of God in the process.

Stating Goals as Behavioral Objectives

Moving from thinking to actual behavior requires the use of behavioral language. The pastoral counselor not only talks about ideas and relationships, he also uses words that describe specific action. Words such as *pray*, *read*, *study*, *say*, and *practice* identify behaviors and not concepts. They focus attention upon actually doing something.

The language of behavior becomes more effective when it is structured around certain categories. Covering as many of these categories as possible is advised. The categories include an action, a specific time, a certain place, and results of the action.

Identify the Results of Behavior

The particular behaviors recommended should be compared to certain negative and ungodly behaviors. This comparison helps to point out the possibility of discouragement. From a theocentric perspective the counselee has been discouraged because he has acted upon priorities that were not centered in God. This sets the stage to appreciate and desire positive and godly behaviors.

Productive and godly results should be emphasized. These serve as reinforcements of theocentric attitudes and habits. The counselee becomes motivated toward effectiveness. Reinforcement comes from the action of God himself in response to the new behavior of the counselee. The pastoral counselor must also provide reinforcement for the new behavior.

Develop Behavioral Steps to Achieve Goals

Behavioral success is more likely if it is set up in short achievable steps. This creates a series of successes. It breaks a monumental task down into manageable units. As each unit goal is accomplished, the counselee is encouraged to continue to the next phase.

Contextual and Developmental
Needs in Theocentric Counseling

This section looks at the impact of context and development upon the pastoral counseling process. The goal of this area is to recognize that God is active in the people and context around the person receiving counsel. The aspects of God which transform methods emphasizing this area are the Incarnation and the work of the Holy Spirit. Through these, God has been active in the world. He continues to be active in the context of individuals' lives. Some of the facets of context are included on the adaptation of the theocentric grid on page 175.

Areas of Context

Context of People, Things, and/or Circumstances	Behavior	Thinking	Emotion	Assumptive/ Spirit
Relationships With People				
Relationships With Institutions				
Circumstances				
Time/Age				
Biological				

Context of Relationships
(Relationship/Lifestyle Skills)

Individuals develop skills for relating to others in the context of family development. The way a person learns to relate to parents and siblings becomes the way that person relates to others in life. As early as 6-8 years of age, a person develops a certain lifestyle approach to relationships based upon the way the child has learned to live with parents and siblings.

Parents and the atmosphere of the home. The atmosphere of morals, values, rules, and boundaries is created in large part by the parents of the home. Children learn how to relate to adults and operate with certain assumptions based upon the actions and skills of the parents in the home. Knowing the atmosphere provided by parents can explain the pressures and nurture a person may or may not have received when lifestyle skills were being formed.

Family of origin and birth order. Birth order—whether a person is born first, second, and so forth, and how close or distant in age siblings are to one another—greatly affects a person's method of approaching life. Before we learn to relate to coworkers, classmates, friends, or associates, we have already learned how to relate to our brothers and sisters. The order of siblings puts them into unique formative relationships that affect the way they develop.

Firstborns tend to be more responsive to authority and more responsible, having been the first one to encounter the parents of the home. Secondborns tend to be more competitive and to seek approval since they always have to contend with an older, stronger sibling. Thirdborns tend to be more open and vulnerable, since they receive more care from parents and older siblings because they are always the younger sibling in need of extra care. The only child may be more apt to seek solitude and attempt to control circumstances because in the absence of other siblings they have more time and opportunity to be alone and work out their own problems.

If siblings are more than four years apart in age, the dynamics of birth order are not as pronounced. Siblings are perhaps inaccessible or distracted by concerns and persons other than younger or older siblings.

Lifestyle approaches. Various lifestyle approaches can result from sibling relationships, birth order dynamics, and the home atmosphere set by parents. Lifestyle approaches have been posited by the work of Wheeler, Kern, and Curlette. They have proposed the following lifestyle approaches which may result from the context of relationships in the early development of an individual. Lifestyle approaches range from the degree that a person likes to be with others or to be alone, whether a person needs to be in charge, the degree to which a person feels a need for recognition, and the level of perfection a person requires of oneself and others.

Early Recollections. Through the use of early recollections, a pastoral counselor can gain insight to sibling relationships and lifestyle approaches that developed as a result. Early recollections are simply the very earliest memories of an individual, usually before the age of 8. Using early recollections does not probe deep into the inner self of a person, nor does it mean looking for some hidden or subconscious meaning. Rather, the pastoral counselor simply looks for the way the person related to others at a very early stage of development. These early patterns may or may not provide insight into current lifestyle approaches.

Context of Relationships (Systems of Relationships)

Family. An important area of context is family relationships. Relationships between husbands and wives and parents and children all affect a person. Family relationships are inescapable. Even if a person has little or no contact with family members, he still has to deal with the fact that he did come from a particular family. Even the absence of one's original family is an issue in itself to be dealt with.

Nonfamily. Another important area of context is nonfamily relationships. These include friends, work associates, and so forth. These relationships may be positive or negative. Regardless, they have some impact upon a person's level of functioning. The pastoral counselor needs to take these along with family relationships into account when dealing with any area of the grid. As illustrated in the diagram, relationships cut across the other areas of the grid.

Church. The impact of church relationships must not be overlooked. The relationships developed within the church form an important bridge with all areas of the grid, especially the area of spirit and primary assumptions. All relationships have an eternal dimension of accountability with God. However, church relationships involve commitments with people who are also believers. The relationships may not be all positive. Nevertheless, they have a strong impact upon the counselee.

Biological Context

Another relationship affecting a person is his biological context. This is his relationship to himself in areas of health and fitness.

Immunological System. An important part of the biological context is the immune system of a counselee. This is his ability to fight off disease. Much of this is accomplished in the body through natural cells which fight off disease. In many cases they literally absorb the disease-carrying cells and agents. This process of absorption and expulsion nullifies the effect of the disease. A person's personal stamina and health in relationship to personal problems does affect his ability to fight off disease. The pastoral counselor can help a person by pointing out the relationship between overall health and how he is responding to a problem.

Neurological System. The neurological system is also an important aspect of the counselee's context. The neurological system involves the reception of stimuli, the processing of information, and the response that is given. The neurological system affects all parts of the body.

Development of the Brain. The biological development of the brain is an important component of the area of context. The brain processes stimuli and responses received from all parts of the body through the neurological system. The functioning of the brain is affected by the health and fitness of the body. It is also affected by the thinking and attitude of the counselee.

Circumstantial Context

Awareness of Events. Events—both good and bad—occurring in the life of a counselee affect his ability to function. These events, which may or may not be within the control of the counselee, can include the loss of a job, an accident, a pay raise, or a natural disaster. The pastoral counselor plays a vital role in helping the counselee respond to these events.

Awareness of Structure of Circumstances. The pastoral counselor can assist a person by helping him to cognitively structure and understand events around him. The structure of events includes their sequence, their cause, and their eventual conclusion. Structuring helps the person gain a sense of control. Awareness of the direction and organization of circumstances can be enhanced through the ministry of the pastoral counselor.

Sociological Contexts (Institutions)

The sociological context of the counselee includes institutions—his job, the government, school, and so forth. The counselee may have positive or negative relationships with these institutions. Much of the work of the pastoral counselor may be in assisting the counselee in adjusting his attitudes toward these institutions. Frequently the counselee is not able to change the institution. But where change is possible, the pastoral counselor may help the counselee in creating godly change. When change is not possible, the counselor may help provide the counselee with coping techniques.

Life Development and Tasks

Life as a Process of Change. Life is in a constant process of change. The circumstances, relationships, and conditions of a person's life do not remain the same. An example is time itself. The progression of time causes aging and change in the counselee's life. An important ministry of the pastoral counselor is helping the counselee adapt effectively to these changes.

Tasks and Transitions. Certain major tasks must be done at each stage of life development.

Stage	Developmental Tasks/Transitions
Infancy	Establishing trust with parents, interaction with the environment
Toddler	Learning to respect limits, determining and communicating basic needs, learning healthy dependency, need for presence of both parents
Preschool	Developing ability to think in relationship to environment, learning and developing language skills, interacting significantly with brothers and sisters
Elementary School	Social development with peers, respecting authority, learning self-discipline
Adolescence	Acquiring sense of identity, establishing roles in relationship to society, accepting changes in body features, developing intellectual skills
Young Adulthood	Finding a spouse, learning to live with spouse, raising children, managing a home, starting an occupation, responsibilities in society
Middle Adulthood	Relating to one's spouse, helping growing children, making an adequate income, community leadership, adjusting to physical decline, adjusting to aging parents

Later Adulthood

Adjusting to aging and death of spouse, establishing satisfactory retirement conditions, accepting identity as aging individual, adjusting to decline in health

Suggestions for Application

The concepts of cognitive, behavioral, and contextual change must be put into practice. The following suggestions are made to enhance that implementation:

1. Use printed materials describing your pastoral counseling ministry. This in itself encourages the counselee toward thinking.

2. Assess and analyze the presence or absence of behavioral words used by the counselee. Using the same words assists him in the thinking process and sets the stage for behavioral change.

3. State behavioral goals, using the behavioral words given earlier by the counselee.

4. Develop a written checklist with the counselee to assure proper follow-up. The written format helps to reinforce the thinking process and actual behavior.

5. Always take into account contextual and developmental factors when assessing other areas of the grid.

6. If the biological context is a factor, recommend that the counselee consult with a physician.

7. Assess the network of relationships in the counselee's life along with other personal factors.

8. Clarify with the counselee the aspects of context and development that are unchangeable. Assist the counselee in seeing God's action in the midst of the process.

PART III

The Application of Pastoral Counseling

Chapter 9

PASTORAL COUNSELING OF FAMILIES AND COUPLES

This chapter introduces important biblical themes concerning the family that can serve as a theological foundation for approaching family issues in counseling. They can also serve as the basis for enrichment and educating the local church about the family. The themes particularly integrate the Christian life and faith with family living.

Relationship Between Personal and Family Commitments (Joshua 24)

In Joshua 24, God first expressed His commitment to the nation and its families. He described all the things He had done for them (v. 13). His blessings, protection, and provision were bountiful. They came expressly from God's love and commitment for His people. They had done little or nothing to receive them.

In response, God asked the nation for its commitment to Him. The Lord used Joshua to pose the question. They were asked to express their commitment and declare whom they would serve (v. 15).

Commitment is often interpreted as an individualistic issue. The assumption is made that people exist by themselves with no family attachments. Decisions and choices are assumed possible without any regard for heritage, home, or responsibilities to others. In particular, individual choices are treated as void of family contingencies.

To the contrary, the commitment asked for in verse 15 is both a personal and family commitment. The two cannot be separated. Individuals do not live completely to themselves. Individual choices always affect others, especially family members. Conversely, family commitments affect its individual members. Joshua expressed his commitment as both a personal and family choice when he said, "As for me and my house, we will serve the Lord."

Spirituality Demonstrated in the Family (Ephesians 5:18—6:4)

In Ephesians 5, Paul described the Christian walk through a series of exhortations. He exhorted the people to walk in love (v. 2), to walk in light (v. 8), to reprove darkness (v. 11), to be spiritually awake (v. 14), to be wise (v. 15), and to be filled with the Spirit (v. 18). The final exhortation was the climax of the series. It was the primary characteristic that especially described the nature of the Christian walk.

Spirituality is illustrated in two ways. Verses 19 and 20 describe spirituality demonstrated in worship. The terms "Speaking and giving thanks" are circumstantial modifiers which are used to amplify the basic exhortation to be filled with the Spirit. The largest section of Paul's discourse, 5:21—6:4, describes the application of spirituality through submissive relationships in the family. The phrase "submitting yourselves" (v. 21) is also a modifier of the exhortation to be filled with the Spirit. Submission applies to everyone. The home is used to illustrate how individuals submit to one another in love, reverence, and obedience (5:33; 6:1).

The size and order of Paul's illustration of the family in this text directly implies that spirituality is especially exhibited through godly relationships in the family. In dealing with spirituality, Paul briefly mentioned worship but used submission within the family to illustrate the Spirit-filled life. If a person is truly spiritual, his spirituality will be lived out in family relationships. If a person does not exhibit proper family relationships, it is a statement about that person's spiritual condition.

Commitment to God's Work in the Family (Ruth)

The Book of Ruth is a family book, not just the story of one woman's commitment. The story begins with the description of a family and the tragedy it experiences (1:1-5). The story first focuses upon the relationship of Ruth and her mother-in-law, Naomi, and later includes another member of the extended family, Boaz. The answer to the calamity of the family is not Boaz's wealth but the birth of a child (4:13-22). The blessing that has come to the family is that the family will not be cut off (4:10).

The temptation is to look at Ruth as an individual and interpret the surrounding events as mere reflections of Ruth. However, the book is about the struggles and near death of a family. The prophetic dimension of the book is that because of the faithfulness of the family—Ruth, Boaz, and Naomi—not Ruth alone, the lineage of David continued and ultimately brought the Messiah. Family faith, not individualistic faith, is the emphasis of the book.

Calamity came to the family, but God did not stop working in their midst. Even in great tragedy, God was still faithful to their family. God used their family as the means by which He would bless them. This is a reminder of God's faithfulness in and through families. The entire family, not just individuals within the family, should in turn respond with praise to the Lord.

Remaining Faithful When a Family Member Is Not Saved (1 Corinthians 7:10-24)

Paul exhorted couples to be faithful to one another. Despite the unfaithfulness of one spouse, he called for the other spouse to remain faithful. Verse 16 especially challenges the believer not to draw presumptuous conclusions about the future condition of the unbelieving spouse.

The theme of faithfulness can be applied to family members in general. The unbelieving family member may be a son, daughter, parent, sibling, or grandparent. The exhortation is to remain faithful to the family member and the family in general.

The exhortations are placed in the context of stewardship in verses 17-24. This is Paul's climactic appeal, taking up much of the section. Faithfulness is an act of stewardship based upon the believer's relationship with God (vv. 17, 22), not the acts or callings of men. The rewards of stewardship are grounded in the Lord. They are not dependent upon the relationship with the unbelieving family member.

Parent-Child Bonding

The parent-child bond is rooted in God's action in forming the family. Human procreation is not dependent merely upon the acts of men and women. Men and women are involved in human reproduction, but the moment of conception is still a miracle wrought by God. It is not subject to chance activity of cells, nor is it dependent solely upon the choices individuals make.

Children are an inheritance from the Lord (Psalm 127:3). An inheritance is not dependent on the worthiness of the recipient. It comes through the benevolence of the donor. The One who gives children is God.

Parent-child bonding is related to the perception of God's gift of children. If children perceive themselves only as the product of human action, the triangle of God, parent, and child is significantly altered. No longer does primary dependence turn toward God. Rather, the child depends first upon the parent. Both the child and the parent feel that their destiny is in their own hands and not in the hands of God. If God is not seen as the origin of the parent-child relationship, He becomes secondary.

This is directly opposite the description of parenting in Psalm 127. In verses 1 and 2 there is an exhortation not to toil in vain. The implication of the context is that the parent toils because he forgets that family and personal responsibilities stem from the benevolence of God. Family responsibilities are real and necessary, but they need not be a burden. The burden and toil comes from forgetting that God has given the family as an inheritance and fruitful reward.

Christ-Centered Life Displayed Through Family Living (Colossians 3:16-21)

Paul emphasized life in Christ in this section of Colossians. He climaxed his appeal by exhorting the believer, "Let the word of Christ dwell in you richly in all wisdom" (v. 16). He stressed the importance of having Christ at the center of one's life.

Paul went on to apply the Christ-centered life to certain spheres of living. The first sphere he mentioned is worship. The latter part of verse 16 identifies the context of worship. In verse 17, he made a general reference to the fact that the Christ-centered life affects all of one's life. His largest illustration is the context of the family (18-21), in which he applied the Christ-centered life to the life of the family.

The evidence of doing "all in the name of the Lord" (v. 17) is especially demonstrated in family living. If a person is allowing Christ to dwell within him richly (v. 16), he will exhibit Christ in the home. The relationships husbands and wives have together, the relationships that parents have with their children, and the relationships children have with parents directly reflect their walk with Christ. If a person is living a Christ-centered life, it will be especially displayed through family living.

Increasing Our Faith Through the Family (Hebrews 11)

Hebrews 11 records many examples of people who had faith in God. These individuals had profound faith whatever their circumstance. When their faith was tested, they allowed God to build even stronger faith within them.

The list reveals that in most of these cases, faith was built in the context of the family. When faith became stronger, it was through the refinery of faith relationships. This indicates that if God is going to build faith and if faith is being tested, it will more than likely occur in the home. There are 20 examples of faith listed in the chapter. Of these, 14 (74%) involve stories of family relationships. The following list reveals this pattern:

Faith Built Through the Family (Hebrews 11)

Verses	Names	Family (numbered)	Faith Area
3	Christians	None explicit	
4	Abel	Two brothers (1)	Faith despite other's failure
5	Enoch	None explicit	Pleased God and was translated
7	Noah	Family (2)	Saving of household
8-12	Abraham, Sarah	Husband, wife (3)	Faith to obey God and bear child
17-19	Abraham, Isaac	Father, son (4)	Faith to give child to God
20	Isaac	Father, two sons (5)	Faith to bless children
21	Jacob	Grandfather, grandsons (6)	Faith to bless grandchildren
22	Joseph	Son, father, grandfather (7)	Faith for godly heritage
23	Amram, Jochebed	Moses' parents (8)	Faith for son's safety
24-26	Moses	Family of origin (9)	Faith to follow family's faith
27	Moses	Son of Pharaoh	Faith despite wrath of the Pharaoh

30	Israelites	None explicit	Faith to conquer Jericho
31	Rahab	Family (10)	Faith for family's safety
32	Gideon	None explicit	Faith to follow God's directions and overcome Midianites
3	Barak	None explicit	Faith to respond to God's call through prophetess Debroah
32	Samson	Delilah, parents (11)	Faith to fulfill calling
32	Jephthah	Son of Gilead, brothers (12)	Faith when rejected by family
32	David	Family (13)	Faith despite personal failure
32	Samuel	Son, mother (14)	Faith for complete dedication

Pastoral Counseling of Couples: Developing the Structure of Love and Honor

Premarital Counseling and Care

Premarital counseling is an excellent opportunity for pastoral counseling. Even if there is some tragic circumstance such as premature pregnancy or sexual promiscuity, the very fact that the couple has now agreed to marriage indicates some degree of commitment. That commitment is an opportunity to minister. The couple are usually excited about their future and are willing to make significant changes in their lives. Pastoral counseling can guide them and at times confront them about the nature and extent of their commitments in marriage.

This book suggests a four-session model for premarital counseling, but the basic issues covered in this proposal can be adjusted to more or fewer sessions. The first session covers several issues: spiritual condition, problems from the couple's perspective, and traits which make for godly marriages. The second session emphasizes the nature and impact of their individual family backgrounds. The third session deals with marital and family roles as defined in Scripture. The final session reviews the wedding ceremony, the honeymoon and wedding night, and the biblical basis of the couple's physical intimacy.

Various emphases need to be made during the sessions. Biblical themes can communicate godly roles for marriage. The perspective of the couple is important because they have their own particular needs. The man and woman each bring to the marriage family issues that represent decades of development. Becoming one does not occur overnight. Working through their own past family histories and integrating their new life together is an important task. Physical intimacy must be addressed from a biblical perspective. The couple can take this opportunity to ask questions they may have little opportunity to ask in the future. They must be assured that this is a godly and fulfilling part of their life together.

The First Meeting With a Married Couple

The first meeting with a married couple is very important because many times a couple does not return a second time. A pastoral counselor may only have one meeting in which to deal with a problem. The couple has usually worked through some apprehension for even one meeting. They may feel anxious about meeting beyond one time. Frequently, they feel satisfied after only one session and never arrange for another meeting. Though the pastoral counselor may think the couple needs more counsel, the couple may not want to meet again.

During the first session there are some goals that deserve consideration. One goal is to hear the perspective of both the husband and the wife. A significant goal is to help them feel an increase in their level of commitment by the time they finish seeing the pastoral counselor, even if only for one time. Another goal is assisting the couple in gaining insight into the nature of their problem. Still another goal is to give the couple specific direction about the issues they are dealing with. A final goal is to place their problems within the context of faith, equipping them to bring their problems to the Lord for His intervention.

The Wish Syndrome of Marriages

The problems couples encounter can be analogous to wishing for many things that are not possible. In marital difficulties there has usually been a sense of loss. Romance, finances, feelings, stability, trust, and so forth, may have been lost in the relationship. Marital counseling can take the form of grief dynamics (see chapter 7). In grief dynamics, an individual may try to deny a loss and wish for a solution that is not possible—for example, wishing that someone had not died.

The wish syndrome of marriages occurs when one, or both, of the partners does not face the reality of the issues and losses they are going through. They wish that things were like they used to be. They wish that problems would go away. They wish that a particular thing had never happened. The wish syndrome can be very damaging because very little, if any, effective change can occur as long as it persists.

There must be a basic admission and agreement between the couple about the problems and issues they are facing. This is a major undertaking in counseling couples. It means changing assumptions and attitudes. It changes the shape of the hopes about the marriage. However, unless the couple can agree on what their problems are, and unless they can admit that those problems exist, resolution is very unlikely. At best, the couple will find some way to cope or "get by" in the meantime. The problem is that many times they find an unscriptural means of coping.

Issues to Identify in Marital Counseling and Care

Issues of family systems of relationships, communication issues, and the relationship of the couple to the larger family are all important. The dynamics of family counseling can apply to the couple's counseling.

There are additional issues to be pursued in working with couples. The couple must deal with learning more-effective ways to communicate with one another. Achieving more understanding of each other's perspective and experience is an important issue. Achieving a deeper sense of unity between one another is significant.

Gaining ability and insight into the emotional needs of each other is helpful. Other issues include flexibility, sensitivity, ability to revise hopes, and gaining skill in working out conflicts. The most significant issues for the couple center on spiritual priorities.

Two basic communication issues deal with the ability to listen to the words and feelings of your partner and then communicating your words and feelings effectively. The problem arises when individuals begin seeing their partner only from their own biased perspective. Also, partners sometimes communicate, caring only to unload what they are feeling without being sensitive to the feelings of the other.

A pastoral counselor can model care and listening. In the meetings he has with the couple, he can listen attentively and then encourage the couple to do the same, especially toward each other. The pastoral counselor can place value upon what each spouse is saying. In turn, he can encourage the couple to place importance and value as well upon what the other partner is wanting to communicate. Unless a couple learns to communicate effectively, it will be hard to address other issues.

Understanding one another and respecting one another is a very important issue when ministering to couples. Frequently husbands and wives confuse the word *clone* with couple. Rather than a marriage partner or a mate, an individual acts as though he wants a clone of himself. There is the expectation that there is only one way to see things, one way to act, and one way to respond—his way. This is a direct violation of God's creation of the uniqueness of an individual. It is a reflection of extreme self-centeredness.

A God-centered perspective understands and respects

the uniqueness of others, especially one's mate. This does not negate right and wrong. However, the rightness or wrongness of something should be seen from God's perspective. Achieving that perspective will lead to mutual understanding under God. The alternative is a self-centered misunderstanding which attempts to make a clone out of one's partner.

Unity in the partnership is an important issue. If the couple has children, they must show unity to the children. They must also show unity to their in-laws and families. This is not to endorse insincerity. It is not an encouragement to pretend there is a unity that does not exist. However, the couple must work out any disagreements in private, not before an audience. The couple must strive to achieve unity.

The ability to share hurts and be emotionally available to one another is important. Many times individuals believe their partner will not care or sincerely feel the weight of their hurts. As a result, they either do not share those hurts with anyone or they share them with others. The pastor can be the one to facilitate the sharing of affections. He can encourage the couple to be open and available to hear each other's hurts.

A critical issue at the heart of marital difficulty is the spiritual condition of the couple. This area cannot be neglected. God is the key to the most effective change for a couple. If the couple's relationship to God is not clarified, then it will be difficult to determine how open they will be to the work of God in their lives. Salvation is a basic requirement for both partners. As the couple matures in genuine spirituality, their ability to grow and overcome issues increases.

Goals for Marital Counseling and Care

A number of overall goals must be kept in perspective when counseling couples. Much of the importance of these goals revolves around spiritual priorities. A central goal is placing first priority upon seeking and maintaining a recognition of God's presence and power in the life of the couple. In connection with this is the goal of being obedient to God's direction and commands to the couple. Another goal is understanding that their commitment to one another is a barometer of their commitment to the Lord.

Another goal is to apply their commitments to the Lord and each other into specific behaviors and changes in their relationship. Yet another goal is to develop new skills and abilities that make for effective marriage. And a final goal is to learn submission to one another in the fear of the Lord.

Pastoral Counseling of Families: Presenting Godly Families Before God

Four Common Family Difficulties

There are some common problems that families encounter. One of these is communication. Families represent a network or system of relationships. This system requires effective communication. A breakdown or distortion in communication affects relationships.

Another common problem is family finance. Finances represent the ability of a family to acquire, manage, and distribute resources. A dysfunction in one or all members of the family in this area affects the goods and services the family is able to manage and receive.

Emotions also contribute to the problems of a family.

People talk with words, but their emotions communicate much more. Emotions become the glue for good or bad between family relationships. Sometimes that bond is so enmeshed that there is no flexibility, only dominance and manipulation.

A final area of problems concerns relationships between parents and children. These problems include the spectrum of irresponsibility all the way to abuse. What is intended by God to be a nurturing relationship turns out to be a selfish, nonnegotiable battle between members of the same family.

There are other family-problem areas. Many of them are related in some way to the four basic areas already mentioned. These other areas include difficulties with in-laws, adjustment to a stage in life development, moving to another area, extramarital affairs, teenage promiscuity, school difficulties, and disciplining the children.

Family as the Most Basic Community Unit

Scripture emphasizes family identity rather than exclusive individual identity apart from family identity. The family origin of individuals is emphasized. Persons are not highlighted for individual identity apart from family idenity. Fathers and mothers are recognized. Family heritage is given a high priority. This is not to create an elitist caste. The purpose is to recognize the reality of the family. People may have had wicked or cruel fathers and mothers, as in the case of Ahab and Jezebel (1 Kings 21). They may have been abandoned, as in the case of Jephthah (Judges 11). Nevertheless, the role of family plays a prominent part in the identity of individuals in Scripture.

The system of the family was important for the life of

the church. This is the reason Paul stressed the importance of family, as mentioned earlier in this chapter. The family of Jesus is mentioned at critical times in the Gospels (John 7:5; 19:25-27). Children were a significant part of Jesus' ministry (Matthew 19:13-15). The family is not ignored or minimized. On the contrary, it was a basic unit of the ministry of Christ and the early church.

The ministry of the pastoral counselor today can do no less than emphasize the critical importance of the family. The life of an individual cannot be separated from the family. Every individual has a family history. Believers must not ignore this reality. A person's family history may be a sensitive issue. The church does not need to share the details of a person's family background. However, believers must not act as though family history does not matter. Pastoral counseling can equip individuals to deal with their family history. Whether that history is good or bad, the believer can commit his family to the Lord. It can become a meaningful part of his testimony.

Central Purpose of the Family and the Will of God

The family as a unit must seek the will of God together. The Lord has a direction for each person within the family. And God is involved in each relationship within the family system. However, the family as a whole must seek God for His will for them as an entire family. God has a message that He desires to communicate through the family together. This was especially recorded in the Old Testament. In particular, the Book of Ruth illustrates this principle. The family of Ruth, Naomi, and Boaz had a message—it was a message of God's mercy and care. God blessed the family and they would continue; their message would not die. In the same way, God desires to speak through family units today.

Pastoral counseling ministry must address the family as a whole. To fail to do so presents too great a priority on individualism. People begin to minimize the importance of the family unit. The family as a whole is left with little or no meaning in the sight of God. On the contrary, pastoral counseling ministry can stress that God desires to speak through the family as a unit. The Lord works for the good of the family as a system of relationships. People view the family as one unit as well as a group of individuals. There is a corporate witness to develop as well as individual testimonies. The pastor-counselor can highlight this process.

The Family Counseling Process

The pastoral counselor has several steps that can be taken in counseling families. Gathering essential family information is necessary to understand the family. Discerning the operation of the family's system of relationships is helpful in seeing how the family functions. The counselor must determine whether the family's difficulties stem from an individual or a relationship within the larger system of the family or whether the family's problems stem from the way the entire family operates. Another key area is monitoring the ability of the family to communicate within the framework of its different relationships. Finally, it is important to identify and monitor the coping level and ability of the family.

The family's history is an important part of the counseling relationship. There are many assumptions that can be made about families in general. The pastoral counselor needs to find out what assumptions can reasonably be made about the particular family he is working with. The best way to particularize information about a family is to search out the history of the family. The most effective way is to make information gathering part of the counseling session. Not only is information gathered, but the pastoral counselor can observe and respond to the way in which the family interprets its history.

There are significant parts of a family's history that the pastoral counselor can ask about. The childhood relationships with parents are important. These relationships form a significant part of present behavior patterns. The behavior observed in a counseling session is due in large part to the way parent-child relationships developed in the past. These include the relationships within the current family. It also includes the kinds of relationships that the father had with his parents and the kinds of relationships the mother had with her parents.

Marriage relationships in the past history of the family are important. Were there many unstable relationships in the past? Did many of the brothers and sisters of the mother and father have stable, Christian marriages? What were the parent-child relationships in these other marriages? These kind of questions help formulate any patterns that may have developed in the family. The impact that these other families may have had on the family the pastoral counselor is currently counseling is especially important.

When looking at parent-child relationships and relationships in other families connected to the family, it is helpful to observe the way these relationships affected the identity and well-being of the family being counseled. These other relationships may have significantly altered or shaped the moral or spiritual nature of the family being counseled. The other relationships may have been adopted as models for relationships. Consciously or unconsciously, specific behaviors or opinions may have been adopted into the family. Knowledge of the impact of these other families upon the family being counseled can be very helpful.

The family's history of involvement with the church is important. A family develops a relationship with church over the course of time. This relationship is usually related to significant events. Identification of the significant events, whether positive or negative, can be helpful. The critical feature to observe is the way in which these events were perceived.

It is impossible to focus completely on what may or may not have happened. However, understanding the way these events affected the family is very important. This kind of insight will not only provide historical information, but the attitude of the family toward spiritual priorities can be detected as well.

Regarding spirituality within the family, it is especially helpful to understand the perception children have had of their parents' spiritual maturity. This includes the perception of children in the family currently being counseled. It also includes the perception that the mother and father have of the spirituality of their mothers and fathers. These perceptions generally have a significant impact upon children. Whether positive or negative, the children had to respond. Their response was based upon their perception of the parents' spirituality. The important issue is not the actual condition of the parents as much as the perception the individual children had.

Much of this information can be gathered while simply recording a time line of the history of the family. The time line can be drawn on a blank piece of paper. It can be drawn up in front of the family. Simply take a piece of paper, draw a single line down the middle. Ask the family about significant dates and events. As they discuss these, place dates and events on the time line in order. The notations need not be elaborate. They may be brief notations. The significance in the time line is not the actual record of events. Rather, the time line is important because it gives the pastoral counselor an accurate picture of this family's own unique history and the way the family views its own history. This insight enables the pastoral counselor to more specifically deal with the family.

The chronology or history of the family can include many significant dates and events. The time line can include births and deaths. The date of marriage is important. Any significant events in the childhood of the mother and father can be important. The courtship of Mom and Dad can provide insight. The circumstances surrounding the birth of each child are important. Any tragedies that may have occurred or any times of blessing can be recorded. The importance of the events mentioned and any events not mentioned cannot be underestimated. One family member may have forgotten something while another family member places extreme importance upon the same event. All of these dynamics can be instructive for the counseling process.

Discerning Basic Functioning of the Family System

The family is a system of relationships. By virtue of their biological or adopted origins, they are related to one another. No matter how good or bad these relationships are, they are nonetheless a relationship and play a significant part in the formation of an individual's personality and character.

There are a number of smaller relationships within the larger relationship of the family. These include the relationship between the mother and father. They also include the relationships between brothers and sisters and between parents and children. To some extent they also include the relationships between extended members of the family such as grandparents, aunts, uncles, and cousins.

All of these relationships function together. They may not function very well. The relationship may be distorted. It may even be abusive. Despite the level, intensity, or health of these relationships, they still function together. They have some level of determination one upon the another.

In the counseling process, the pastoral counselor must discern the nature and level of functioning between these relationships. Observation of the way in which parents relate to each other, children relate to one another, and parents and children relate is important. Insight into these relationships when counseling families is as important as, if not more important than, seeing differences within individuals. Family problems stem from relational difficulties as much as, if not more than, they stem from personal problems.

Construction of a Family "Genogram"

One effective way to record family functioning is to construct a family tree, or "genogram." This can be done on a blank piece of paper. Individual members of the family can be symbolized with lines drawn to attach them. Other family members such as grandfathers and grandmothers can be identified. Birth dates, dates of deaths, significant information, and so forth, can be noted next to specific names. The genogram can be drawn in front of the family, while talking with them. It can become a counseling tool. Issues and perspective can be gained while recording the genogram.

Determine the Emphasis of a Problem

Problems can be centered in an individual or they can affect the entire family. A husband may be dealing with a personal issue that has only a minor effect on his wife or children. An example might be a theological issue or question. At other times, a person may have a problem that is affecting him greatly. He may think it does not affect his family, but it does. An example would be a conflict at work. The husband brings the conflict home through carryovers in attitude and emotions. He may think it is not affecting his family, but it is.

The pastoral counselor must discern whether a problem is more individual or family-related. The counseling concerns for individuals vary. If it is an individual issue, individual counseling may be more appropriate. If it is a family issue, family counseling is the most effective approach. In individual counseling, family issues may be related. They can be addressed in the context of individual counseling. However, if it is actually a family issue, addressing it merely as an individual issue could be counterproductive. The whole family should be involved in the counseling and caring process.

Monitor Family Communication Skills

In observing the family, the pastor can carefully observe the way the family communicates with one another—certainly the content of what is being said. The actual substance of the conversations and the emotional communication taking place are important. The emotional communication is especially insightful. Individuals not only say words, but they feel their words. These emotions in communications can be observed through verbal and nonverbal indicators. Verbal indicators would include words, inflections, and pitch of the voice. Nonverbal indicators could include gestures, posture, and distance. All of these kinds of observations help the pastor gain insight into the manner and level of communication between family members.

Family Members Often Create a Scapegoat

Often, in communicating and relating to one another, family members may scapegoat another member of the family. A scapegoat bore the sins of the community in the Old Testament. In similar fashion, family members may place blame, negative emotions, or pressure they feel upon a certain member of the family. Frequently, everyone in the family may choose the same scapegoat. For example, Mom and Dad may feel bad toward one another about a financial problem. At the same time, they may feel afraid to show their negative emotions about one another. Both of them would then unload those negative emotions upon their son while talking to him about his school problems. This kind of transfer of emotions upon the same person is scapegoating. Everyone else feels better because they are not carrying around those emotions. But the scapegoat has to feel the weight of what everyone else has dumped on him.

Assessment of the Family's Level of Coping

Families develop ways of dealing and coping with stress. When a crisis or problem arises in the family, the family responds with certain ways of coping. These coping mechanisms develop over the course of time. They are passed on from family to family. They may be the result of some new influence upon the family. A family may develop a new way of coping in response to a new kind of problem.

There are a variety of ways that families learn to cope. These may be positive or negative. They may be godly or ungodly. The common thread is that these are things families use in order to adjust to problems and crises.

Some of the positive and godly ways of coping include times when the family responds by drawing closer to the Lord. They may seek the help of a friend or the pastor. The family may take a brief vacation or trip. They may have learned to sit down and work on the problem together. There may be an overall increase in devotion, prayer, and Bible study.

At other times families may cope in negative or ungodly ways. The family members may isolate themselves from one another. Some families feel they cope best by yelling and screaming. Other families may isolate or scapegoat one particular member of the family. Sometimes abuse is used as a coping method.

Identification of the family's coping style assists the pastoral counselor in the counseling process. The counselor may focus on new methods of coping. The good coping methods the family has may be emphasized. The absence of any coping tends to create a real crisis situation, and identification of this void could be used by the counselor for counseling. The counselor may simply give the family an assessment of the coping resources they have and those they do not have. This kind of awareness may be new for the family. It can give them insight about changes they need to make.

Suggested Methods for Guiding Change in Families

The immediate concern of the pastoral counselor in family counseling is to get the entire family in for counseling. If the problem is one that affects the whole family to a significant degree, the whole family needs to come together for counseling. Some of the children may be older and have moved out of the home. If the issues do not currently involve them, they would not need to come to see the pastoral counselor. However, the family members who are being affected need to come in for counsel.

If the problem mainly involves only one or two relationships within the family, then that portion of the family can come to see the counselor. However, if the whole family is being affected, they all need to come. This is the first methodological step.

Some methods of assessment have already been mentioned. Writing out a family time line is helpful. Drawing a family tree or genogram is insightful. Observation of the way the family functions has also been mentioned.

Methods of family counseling need to be directed toward specific goals. Family issues are very complex, but this does not mean that specific goals cannot be made. These goals may not address all of the problems. However, they will approach many of the critical issues. An important method is to write down these goals. This ensures that they are specific enough to be remembered.

They become common for all the family. Write down goals and share them with the family.

Written exercises before, during, and after counseling can be helpful. One exercise could be writing down personal goals for the family. The family could also draw pictures and images of their family. Drawing a diagram of their family at work or play may be insightful. Before and after counsel, family members can be given scriptures to study. It may be helpful to ask the family to write down thoughts and issues that arise during the week. These can be brought to the pastoral counselor for his prayer and counsel. Writing and committing to a covenant can be a powerful tool.

The Pastoral Counselor's Family

The pastoral counselor must first address his own family. The counselor's family will have its own set of problems. Not everyone in the family may be saved. However, the reaction and relationships the pastoral counselor has with his own family is important. This task takes first priority in his ministry to families in the church. The pastoral counselor must not have the unrealistic goal of having the "perfect family." The pastoral counselor cannot make everyone in his family become a Christian. However, the pastoral counselor can control the way he relates to his family.

The way in which a pastoral counselor relates to his spouse and his family sets the tempo for his ministry. The relationship style of the pastoral counselor is most critically tested in the home. He may appear one way to people in ministry, but he may act another way at home. The way he acts at home is a more significant barometer of his character than the way he acts in public.

Frequently, the pastoral counselor's family is placed under a lot of pressure. It is expected to be a perfect, flawless family. The pastoral counselor's children come under heavy condemnation because they do not act according to the perceptions and expectations of members in the church. This kind of pressure is unfortunate, unrealistic, and wrong.

However, despite the undue criticism made of a pastoral counselor's family by immature believers in the church, the pastoral counselor's family does serve as a witness to others. Even though the family is not perfect, it can still be in the process of growth in Christ. Even though every family member may not be saved, the other family members can bear a burden for the salvation of those that are lost. Although the pastoral counselor's family cannot exhibit perfection, they can communicate their care, love, and concern for one another. This can provide a strong witness of God's love and care working in a family.

Principles for Application

The principles of Scripture must be used as foundational material for addressing family problems. In order to apply this chapter, the following suggestions are made:

1. List certain family issues that may be addressed by the principles listed in this chapter.

2. Develop additional themes for other issues that may arrive.

3. Involve the entire family in counseling when the entire family is affected by the issue.

4. Sponsor an annual or regular enrichment conference for families you are counseling. It could be a couples retreat for those in the local church.

5. Develop a specific format for premarital counseling.

6. Recognize the importance of the first session with a couple. Clarify your desire to meet more than once if you feel it would be in their best interest.

7. Develop a biblical list of priorities for couples and use it as a counseling tool.

8. At important times when counseling couples, clarify for them how you see the unique perspective of each of them.

9. When you see the wish syndrome or "clone" tendency, inform the couple of the pattern you believe you are seeing.

10. Effectively share the importance of the spiritual aspect with the couple, clarifying the way in which the ability to change is minimized if there is not a strong level of spiritual maturity.

11. Develop some personal guidelines and procedures for your counseling ministry to families.

12. Develop statements and materials to be included in publications which articulate the kind of commitment you have as a pastoral counselor to families.

13. If you are a part of a local church ministry, integrate ministries to different age groups into an organizational strategy which emphasizes the unity of the family. Organizational charts and group names can include statements about the unity of the family. Sometimes the specialization of different age groups can communicate a fragmented picture of the family.

14 .Involve parents in meetings with teachers and youth ministers.

15. Address the special needs of those whose children are grown. Stress that the family does not end when the children have grown up.

16. Determine to keep the schedule of your own personal family as your first priority in ministering to other families.

17. Develop the health of your own family. Your reactions to them form the basis for your reactions to other families.

18. Use the time line and genogram as regular family-counseling tools.

19. Clarify to those you counsel whether you feel this is a family or personal matter. Then proceed with either personal or family counseling.

20. Determine that if there is a scapegoat in a family, you will minister special care for that person.

Chapter 10

PASTORAL COUNSELING IN CRISIS SITUATIONS

Three areas of pastoral counseling will be covered in this chapter—an "actual crisis," stress, and burnout/impairment. An "actual crisis" represents an acute, immediate failure to cope. Stress represents the responses of an individual to demanding situations and relationships. Burnout and impairment represent the more long-term implications of pressured living.

Actual Crisis

A crisis can be characterized in five different ways. One characteristic is a sense of hopelessness and failure. A second characteristic is a sense of panic. There is an accompanying fearfulness about the failure to cope with the crisis. A third characteristic is some degree of physical symptoms. These range from nervous habits and hyperactivity to exhaustion and depression. The fourth characteristic is a focus on relief. The individual just wants an immediate solution and relief from the pressure. The final characteristic is lowered efficiency. A person may be able to function on the job and at home, but the level of efficiency is much lower.

Changes in one or more of three primary areas may precipitate a crisis. These are perception, relationships, and coping mechanisms. Perception is the personal perspective a person has about a situation or relationship. Relationships include persons that normally help to support a person. Coping mechanisms are the various behaviors and attitudes a person has developed to deal with problems. When one or more of these three fail to function, a crisis is likely to occur. What may have worked before no longer works for the individual. The morality of these three areas may not have been godly, but the person has used them to survive. In the case of ungodliness, God may be using a crisis to change a person's use of one of these.

A crisis is to be distinguished from ongoing pressures. Complete failure to function in one or more of the three areas mentioned—perception, relationships, and coping mechanisms—marks an actual crisis. In mere pressure a person is still able to use these three areas as before. The content of an issue or relationship does not dictate whether an actual crisis is occurring. The person's ability to perceive, relate, and cope in the midst of these pressures determines whether crisis proportions have been reached. This chapter deals with intervening in actual crisis situations.

The Context of Precrisis and Postcrisis Issues

In the events leading up to an actual crisis, a series of events can usually be seen. There is typically one event which initiated the events that led up to the actual crisis.

The initiating event may seem like an irony and serves only as a catalyst—"the straw that broke the camel's back." The path leading to a crisis is usually a matter of people and events, not ideas. The pastoral counselor will understand precrisis development better by focusing on individuals and events. Particularly helpful is finding a series of "firsts." "Firsts" are the first times that feelings of failure and panic began to happen.

Postcrisis events relate to recovery after the crisis. Referral and continued support are important. The pastoral counselor can assist the person in not slipping back into crisis. Growth can take place if the person has reacted well to the actual crisis. This does not mean the absence of tragedy or pain. Rather, after the impact of the crisis has subsided, rebuilding can effectively take place.

Methods for the Actual Crisis

In the midst of the actual crisis, it is important to be direct. The duration of an actual crisis may not be very long. Therefore, it is important to make every moment as effective as possible. If it is an actual crisis, the person has lost the ability to cope. Strong, direct intervention is necessary. The skill in pastoral counseling is to be direct without domineering. Definite directions for action must be given. Decisive insight must be conveyed to avoid further danger or damage.

When approaching the actual crisis, assessment of the precrisis development is important. This assessment will give direction for the crisis intervention. It will tell the pastoral counselor who is involved. It will also tell him what resources are available. It is especially important to determine what the initiating event that triggered the crisis was. Ultimately, resolution of the initiating event is the first major key for crisis reduction.

The pastoral counselor is usually more involved in monitoring than making actual changes in the midst of a crisis. The person is in a condition of near panic. As a result, change cannot be forced. The person is already very volatile and fragile. The pastoral counselor must seek to initiate change while monitoring the counselee's response to efforts to change. The crisis will not subside until the counselee himself changes. These changes are more monitored than forced.

The time of an actual crisis is relatively short. As a result, the pastoral counselor must develop a short-term response. Goals for intervention should be simple and achievable. It may be as brief as separating two partners in conflict into separate rooms. It may be as practical as a phone call to communicate an important message. Whatever the particular strategy, it must be very short-term. This requires a focus upon the precrisis events and actual crisis. Prolonged deliberation about issues and relationships that have been longer in development—that is, ongoing problems—will not solve the immediate crisis.

Immediate action is highly desirable when responding to an actual crisis. The counselee has lost perception, relationships, and/or coping mechanisms. As a result, any hesitancy to develop an immediate response only compounds the sense of panic and failure. The short-term response of the pastoral counselor should include some type of specific behavior and action. This assures the counselee of some hope for recovery from the immediate crisis. Immediate actions may include getting something to eat, making a person comfortable, taking someone into another room, making an important phone call, or coming immediately to the scene of the crisis.

Criteria When Responding to Crises of Severe Physical Abuse

When a counselor is dealing with the crisis of physical abuse, a change usually occurs in the nature of the pastoral counselor's relationship with the counselee. Both the abuser and abused may have a very reactive kind of personality. As a result, they may react strongly to the reality that the abuse is going to be addressed by the pastoral counselor. A change in the relationship between counselor and counselee may not occur. However, the pastoral counselor needs to be prepared for a wide variety of responses.

The pastoral counselor must have adequate information when responding to a crisis, especially the crisis of extreme physical abuse. If there is adequate information to confirm abuse, then action must be taken. However, if there is not sufficient physical evidence and corroborating information, action should not be taken. If action is taken only on the basis of one person's account, he may change his story. It is best to seek for some tangible, objective kind of physical evidence that actual abuse was the cause of damage.

The pastoral counselor should develop consulting relationships with doctors, health-care professionals, police officers, and so forth. These are the kinds of relationships that are helpful when referrals, consulting, and reporting must be done. The decision about whether actual abuse is taking place is an important one. It is very helpful if the decision can be made in consultation with others.

The pastoral counselor should secure copies of state

and local statutes pertaining to abuse and the reporting of that abuse. The best source is the state agency which handles such information. The information should be current because laws may change from year to year. A phone call directly to the agency at the state capital is usually the best way to secure such information.

Physical safety of the abused is the first priority. The pastoral counselor should take immediate action if he is absolutely convinced of abuse and has firm evidence of such abuse. Regardless of the action, safety is the first and overriding concern. This usually means getting the abused to a safe place. The pastoral counselor should be cautious, especially if there is no firm and corroborating evidence. However, once such evidence is available, safety is a must.

Stress

Pastoral Counseling of Individuals Experiencing Stress

Stress occurs when there is an inequality in the amount of perceived resources to handle stress and the perceived demands a person faces. The concept of perception indicates the importance of how a person individually views resources and demands. For example, the same demand may be viewed differently by two people. One person may not feel that there is an unreasonable demand, while another may feel the demand is overwhelming. Resources can also be perceived differently. A particular way of approaching a demand may be seen as an effective resource by one person but rejected by another. When the perception of resources is smaller than the perception of demands, stress is created.

Kind of Demands That Can Produce Stress

Stress is not necessarily a bad thing. It can prove to be a motivator if occurring in a certain quantity. Such stress is called *eustress*, meaning "good stress." At other times stress can definitely be a negative influence. In such cases it is known as *distress*. The amount of stress can also be a factor. Too much or too little stress can become a negative factor. There is an optimal level of stress for everyone. At the optimal level a person receives enough stress to provide effective motivation.

Certain events in life are stressful. The following are items from a list developed by Thomas Holmes and Richard Rahe. They include the 10 most stressful events individuals encounter: death of a spouse, divorce, marital separation, detention in jail, death of a close family member other than spouse, major personal injury, marriage, being fired from work, marital reconciliation, and retirement from work.

Specific Resources for Dealing With Stress

There are several possible resources the pastoral counselor can focus on. These can be developed by the counselee. The counseling relationship can be the vehicle by which these are identified and developed. The following definitions are adopted from stress studies, especially the work of Matheny, Curlette, Aycock, Pugh, and Taylor.

Self-disclosure is the ability to open up and communicate one's feelings, ideas, hopes, troubles, and so forth. This skill allows a person to develop trust and interpersonal skills with others. It also develops a feeling of sharing the weight of a stressful event or relationship. If a person is not good at self-disclosure, he will develop distrust and limit his ability to find options.

Self-directedness is the level of confidence a person has about his ability to make judgments and assessments. This relates to the ability to discern the critical elements of stressors and respond confidently and effectively. The lack of self-directedness creates an inhibiting tentativeness about combating the effects of stress.

Confidence relates to the overall perception of the individual about the ability to overcome stress. An effective level of confidence is realistically in touch with a person's true success in overcoming a stressor. A lack of confidence may create a negative environment in which the effects of stress are compounded and made increasingly worse.

Acceptance relates to the person's ability to overcome stress through the use of relationships. Others become resources for stress management. A person is not afraid to ask for help and is able to help others. It also indicates a certain flexibility with other people as resources for coping with stress. A lack of acceptance means a person is demanding or distant regarding others, unable to receive assistance in coping with stress.

Social support refers to a person's availability to others. It means that a person deals with stress by mutually giving and receiving help from others. While acceptance focuses upon flexibility in relationships, social support focuses upon availability in relationships. A lack of social support means that a person responds to stress by withdrawing from others.

Ability with finances as a resource for stress indicates effective money management. It does not necessarily refer to the amount of money a person may have. The lack of ability creates greater stress, regardless of the amount of money a person may have.

Physical health refers to the actual condition of a person's body. If a person is in good health, then his body is able to respond with physical stamina to the pressures that stress can create. Poor physical health can either create or compound stress.

Physical fitness differs from physical health. Fitness refers to the lifestyle habits of a person which may affect health. Fitness habits can help a person combat the effects of stress even if his overall health is not the best, while poor fitness skills degenerates health as well as compounds any effects of stress.

Stress awareness and monitoring is the ability of the person to be alert to and respond to stress. Individuals high in this skill are able to identify events or relationships as being stressful. They are aware when stress affects health and normal functioning. Correspondingly, this skill means that a persons has learned how to effectively respond to the effects of stress. A person low in this skill will be tossed about emotionally by stress, unaware of the source.

Tension control is a specific application of stress awareness. In this skill a person is able to make adjustments in lifestyle and habits in order to take on the effects of a stressor. A person is aware and has access to resources and relationships that can control the sources of tension which might create stress. The absence of tension control allows for tension to mount up until events and relationships reach stressful levels.

Functional beliefs is the most critical of the coping resources for the pastoral counselor. This resource emphasizes the role of faith and one's belief system. A person responds to stress by first relying on God as the primary resource. The Lord gives direction and strength to apply all of the other resources. The pastoral counselor functions to facilitate the use of faith in responding to stress.

Burnout/Impairment

The Lord seeks to revive and refresh an individual. The believer, even under great duress, is able to find resources for effective coping through his relationship with the Lord. The lack of personal faithfulness often results in burnout. When the central priority of personal devotion to God is changed, all other priorities of a person's life are moved out of order, resulting in stress and burnout.

Burnout is not defined by the amount of energy a person may or may not use. Individuals have varying degrees of available energy. Just because a person may or may not work hard does not mean that he is experiencing burnout. Burnout is not simply running short on energy or stamina. It is not the same as tiredness.

Fatigue and stress become burnout when they begin to affect a person's ability to function in necessary ways. This is called "impairment." He may not be able to work as long and as effectively as before on the job. The person may not be able to perform necessary tasks at home. He may not be able to maintain relationships with other individuals who are significant to him.

The Phases of Burnout

There are critical elements, or phases, in the development of burnout. These symptoms may occur at any time and in any order. These phases simply represent trends and stages in the development of burnout. The central cause for these conditions is often a lack of personal devotion to God and applying that devotion in areas of rest and effective motivations. The result is impairment in required functioning.

First Phase: Extreme Enthusiasm

This initial phase is marked by extreme enthusiasm. The individual is very motivated. There is some measure of early success. It is a time of zeal and strong hope. The trend toward burnout occurs when the zeal and thrill of success itself becomes more important than essential priorities. The most important of these is personal devotions. Other priorities that are neglected include family, personal leisure, and fitness.

Second Phase: Stagnation

Stagnation occurs when early success no longer occurs as frequently and disillusionment sets in. Failures and the inability to succeed in any one thing does not necessarily create tension. However, repeated and mounting failure creates a sense of annoyance.

A person begins to recognize that initial hopes are not being realized. Actual stagnation in the form of burnout sets in when the person persists in the misalignment of priorities. Each effort to reinforce a misplaced priority results in a stagnated, ineffective attempt. This phase is especially marked by bewilderment about unmet expectations.

Third Phase: Frustration

Frustration occurs in the cycle of burnout when the individual begins to discover how futile his attempts become. It appears that the person is without the power and authority needed to accomplish previously set goals and hopes. The problem rests with the misplaced priorities established in the initial stage of enthusiasm.

The person focuses on power which he feels he needs but does not have. Increasingly, he feels as though his misdirected priorities will never be met. The power to return to initial levels of enthusiasm seems more and more out of reach. However, burnout is perpetuated in a constant but futile search. A mark of this stage is the feeling that no one cares about the individual's condition or frustrated dreams.

Fourth Phase: Apathy

Apathy occurs when burnout progresses to emotional detachment from one's misplaced priorities and hopes. While the individual does not give up trying to fulfill these, he has lost the heart to try. He is merely a shell seeking to survive. The focus of attention is survival.

Initial zeal which started the burnout cycle has now turned to bitterness and withdrawal. In fact, the earlier dreams resulting from extreme enthusiasm now serve as a source of torment. This phase is the longest in developing, and it takes the longest time to overcome.

Fifth Phase: Hopelessness

Hopelessness can occur in varying degrees at any stage. In this stage, however, the person loses all hope connected with the initial stage of extreme enthusiasm. He will not rediscover the central priority of personal faithfulness to God; neither will he revive other important priorities such as the family. Rather, the person chooses to remain without hope.

Pastoral Counseling for Those Experiencing Burnout

Burnout and impairment can occur to anyone in the community of faith. Pastors and ministers can become disillusioned and burned-out. Christian lay workers can become burned-out in Christian service. There is a tremendous need for pastoral counselors to serve as healers and interveners for those experiencing burnout.

The best time to intervene is between the stages of frustration and apathy. Intervention is difficult in the early stages because "successes" with misplaced priorities cloud the counselee's ability to clearly see needs in his life. Intervention is difficult once the counselee arrives at apathy because there is little motivation to change. However, at the level of frustration the counselee has a better opportunity to see the need for turning around and still has some measure of motivation to do so.

An important step is to clarify the issues involved in burnout. This gets the counselee to think about his condition. Much of the time, he has been reacting primarily with emotions. Clarification of issues encourages the counselee to move from a merely reactive condition to a more effective problem-solving one. The issues involved include a return to personal devotion and seeking the priorities God may place in his life, other misplaced and/or neglected priorities, adjusting initial hopes, and being flexible to changing circumstances.

Developing a healing relationship is important for the wounded emotions of the person experiencing burnout. The pastoral counselor should be aware of these wounded emotions, battered by the process of burnout. Merely feeling that someone cares is a decisive step in the counseling and recovery process.

The pastoral counselor should assist the counselee in reviving his stamina and resources. The counselee is probably exhausted from the stress and tension of burnout. A planned time of refreshment and physical replenishing is important. This time of refreshing contributes to the physical health and fitness of the counselee.

A "decompression routine" is an intentional time of moving away from the priorities that are secondary to the priorities that are more important. The secondary priorities must be addressed and monitored. However, the counselee must learn what areas of his life are more important and how to revert back to these on a regular basis. For example, while coming home from the job or place of ministry, the counselee can go through a routine of laying aside the events of the day and determine to place a priority on what will be occurring at home.

Recovery from burnout usually requires deliberate intention on the part of the counselee. The counselor must assist the counselee in developing a motivation and desire for change. The recovery process will be hard work, running counter to emotions that have been developed over the course of time. However, with the right amount of intentional action, recovery is possible.

Suggestions for Application

The following suggestions are made for counseling individuals experiencing crisis, stress, or burnout:

1. Be able to identify the warning signs and characteristics of an actual crisis.

2. Develop crisis intervention around the three areas of perception, relationships, and/or coping mechanisms.

3. Focus immediately upon developing rapport and

relationship. The fact that the pastoral counselor is present establishes the first step in relationship.

4. Build relationships with consulting professionals who can assist you with crisis cases.

5. Obtain printed copies of the laws pertaining to abuse and other crisis issues.

6. Help an individual understand the relationship between stress and the perception of stress.

7. Identify the various sources of stress.

8. List various events in the recent experience of the counselee which may have been sources of stress.

9. Guide the counselee in identifying resources he currently has for responding to stress.

10. Monitor your own potential for burnout, especially maintaining the central and first importance of personal devotion to God.

11. Help a counselee see the particular stage of burnout he may be experiencing.

12. Assist the counselee in a regular "decompression routine," offering practical suggestions and options of times for such a routine, for example, while in the car, when first coming home, when taking the last break on the job, and so forth.

13. Try to reach an individual before he reaches the stage of apathy. If he has not yet reached apathy, it is worth the effort perhaps to confront him about his condition.

Chapter 11

PASTORAL COUNSELING WITH SPECIAL METHODS FOR EFFECTIVENESS

Brief and One-Session Pastoral Counseling

At times the pastoral counselor may not be able to counsel someone very many times. The person may only want to come once or twice. The counselee may be embarrassed about the topic discussed. The person may feel like counseling is no longer needed after a few sessions. It may be a crisis situation in which there is only time for one or two sessions. Whatever the reasons for limiting the amount of counseling, the counselor can still make these brief occasions effective.

Pastoral counseling does not have to be lengthy to be effective. When the right words are used at the right time in the right way, counseling can be effective. The effectiveness of counseling may level out after five to eight sessions. In fact, the pastoral counselor must be prepared to make the first session one of the most effective because as many as 50 percent of individuals coming for counseling do not return for a second session.

The pastoral counselor does not have to assume that counseling done in a briefer span of time is necessarily less effective. Quite often, waiting for effectiveness in later counseling means a missed opportunity, because the individual or couple may not return.

Methods for brief counseling must be solution-focused. When the counselee comes for counsel, the pastoral counselor should assess the major problem confronting the counselee. The counselee may discuss a variety of topics. However, the pastoral counselor must search for root issues and a single theme that needs to be addressed. The best source of information is usually the counselee. Simply ask the counselee what is the major concern according to his perception that needs to be addressed.

Brief pastoral counseling should focus upon current issues. Exhaustive analysis into the past of the individual is time-consuming. At times, more thorough analysis is needed. However, solving the immediate problem of the counselee requires a here-and-now focus.

The problem brought to light for a solution usually involves current issues, perspectives, and relationships. The pastoral counselor must immediately address these issues. Distractions into side issues and secondary concerns should be minimized. A major part of the counseling task is finding a relevant here–and–now focus and maintaining it.

Identifying Goals

An effective way of approaching problems is to look at the kind of thinking and perception that has led to the problem. Behind a problem is usually a certain set of assumptions and thoughts. There are some problems which did not originate in the perception of the counselee. However, even in these cases, the perception of the counselee is an important component to the current impact of the problem. It is also related to the way in which the counselee will deal with the problem now. The pastoral counselor must find the thoughts, attitudes, and perceptions which affected the formation of the problem.

A vital part of brief pastoral counseling is empathizing with the counselee. Empathy emphasizes the feelings of the person. Many times the counselee is in a crisis situation. At other times there are pressures upon the counselee. The nature of the circumstances creates strong emotions in the counselee, and the pastoral counselor must minister to these emotions.

Empathy must be accomplished in a relatively short period of time. The pastoral counselor can care for the counselee without condoning inappropriate actions or attitudes of the counselee. The level of effectiveness is related to the level of care. And care can still be given even though time may be limited.

Goals for brief pastoral counseling need to focus on specific behaviors. If some behavioral change can be observed, the counselor will feel a greater sense of accomplishment. It will also demonstrate progress in any work that has been started in the areas of spirit, emotions, and/or thinking. Frequently, the counselee is looking for some tangible, visible sign of improvement. A change in behavior provides for this need.

The counselee and others involved with him can see and experience the change in behavior. The behavioral change would probably be accompanied by emotional and spiritual change as well. It may not be. However, the likelihood of more complete change taking place in the life of the counselee is increased when behavior is actually changed. Behavioral goals and changes can be achieved in a relatively short period of time.

What Is Not Working

One of the initial steps in brief pastoral counseling is to identify what is not working at the present time. Most often, the counselee will begin by emphasizing the negative. There is frequently an extensive list of several factors and issues that are not working well for him.

The pastoral counselor should try to reduce the list to the most critical issues facing the counselee. Of this list, the most pressing matter that is not working for the counselee should be identified. This process gives the pastoral counselor and the counselee a fairly good idea of situations, attitudes, emotions, and behaviors to avoid. The pastoral counselor can refer to the avoidance of these as counseling progresses.

What Is Working

After analyzing what is not working for the counselee, the pastoral counselor should identify what is working. The counselee may not feel like anything is working for him. He may feel like nothing is going right. However, the pastoral counselor can carefully ask about anything that is pleasant, restful, rewarding, and so forth, in the life of the counselee. Also, the pastoral counselor can ask whether the negative factors in his life are experienced literally 24 hours a day with no break. Usually, there is at least some remnant of positive experience and/or break in negative factors. These items form the basis for developing what is working in the life of the counselee.

Adapting What Works

The pastoral counselor should adapt what is working for the counselee into the circumstances of what is not working. This is an important process in brief pastoral counseling. For example, if a counselee is experiencing some very difficult circumstances at home in the evenings but feels very good early in the mornings, the pastoral counselor could try to help the counselee bring some of the factors experienced in the morning into the evening time at home. The positive factors in the morning may include rest, quiet, a good meal, and devotional time. These factors could be reproduced for the evening setting. Adapting factors is a very effective way of providing some guidance for individuals in a brief amount of time.

Godly Affirmation

The pastoral counselor must stress a God-centered perspective in the brief counseling process. The action and intervention of God is at the center of the process. The perception of the pastoral counselor is very important. He must see God moving from the very beginning and throughout the process. The steps reviewed in Part II about theocentric methodology are possible even in brief periods of time. The various concerns discussed in this chapter, including identification of goals and focusing on what works, must all be directed by the pastoral counselor's perception of the action of God in the midst of the process.

Accountability and Follow-up

The pastoral counselor should set up a time of follow-up and accountability. This assures that the effects of the brief time of counseling will be monitored. Accountability can be maintained through follow-up visits, written homework (to be discussed later in this chapter), establishing relationships with others who can help the counselee, assignment of specific tasks that can be monitored, and a variety of other means.

Pastoral counseling during brief opportunities does not necessarily diminish the effectiveness of the counseling. The pastoral counselor must be aware of special needs and methods relating to brief counseling. This is especially true because so many people come for only one session of counseling.

Writing for Effective Change

The Bridge From Feelings to Actions

A common problem in pastoral counseling is to help a person move from feelings to actions. The counselee may have very deep hurts. He may be able to share those hurts with the pastoral counselor. The pastoral counselor may be able to empathize and minister to those hurts. However, the counselee also needs to move beyond those hurts to actions. His behavior must reflect the change in his heart. He must begin to act upon the positive and godly emotions that have just experienced healing.

On the theocentric grid used earlier, thinking stood between actions and emotions. That position illustrates that thinking is the bridge between emotions and actions. If the pastoral counselor can guide the thought process of the counselee, this will help focus the emotional change into effective behavior. Writing is an important method for encouraging the counselee to think.

Using writing as a method of pastoral counseling is important because writing is an important way to help counselees think about changes they need to make. The act of writing requires thinking. It represents the process of the mind applied to a specific topic. This process of thinking facilitated by writing eventually leads to changes in behavior. In fact, writing itself is a behavior. It becomes the first of many behavioral changes that can occur.

Benefits of Writing

There are many benefits to writing as part of pastoral counseling. The following list of benefits is an adaptation of benefits listed by Waylon O. Ward in his book *The Bible in Counseling:*

1. The thinking of the counselee is redirected.
2. New insights are received.
3. Insights gained in counseling are reinforced.
4. Dependency is established upon God because the counselee is working away from the presence of the pastoral counselor.
5. Comfort and support established in the counseling session can be extended through concepts assigned in written assignments.
6. More information can be communicated beyond the counseling time.
7. Good habits and discipline are established.
8. Changes in attitude, perception, behavior, and so forth, can be measured.
9. The counselee becomes involved in Bible study.
10. Communication skills are developed.
11. Writing creates a sense of hope and accomplishment.

Additionally, as the counselee receives affirmation and guidance from the counselor, a greater sense of control over his problems is achieved.

An important aspect of written approaches to pastoral counseling is designating a specific time. A designated time must be set aside by the counselee for working on written assignments. Specifying the time provides the counselee with boundaries and requirements. Frequently, problems have arisen in the life of the counselee because of a failure to abide by limitations and requirements. The issue of a specific time to write becomes a tool to develop a sense of submission and order for the counselee. The content of the written assignment is important in itself, and specifying a time for writing reinforces the content by relating it to the lifestyle of the counselee. The particular time can be mutually agreed upon by the pastoral counselor and the counselee.

Another important issue related to time is the routine of the assignment. The specified time should be at the same time each day. This routine is a powerful source of reinforcement. It creates an adjustment in the lifestyle of the counselee. Whereas he may have felt controlled by a particular problem, he now is able to direct his attention toward resolution of that problem as a part of his regular lifestyle and habit. Integrating the content of the written assignment into the life and habits of the counselee through the routine of the assignment is an important part of the counseling process.

The written assignments used by the pastoral counselor should be designed to address the needs of the counselee. The following format for developing written homework assignments is adopted from Luciano

L'Abate's book *Programmed Writing:*

1. At the beginning, do not worry about size.
2. Have an overall outline of several assignments.
3. Avoid lengthy instructions.
4. Build regular, behavioral tasks into each lesson.

The writing assignment should incorporate aspects of faith and Scripture. Some forms of written assignments include diaries, journals, Bible studies, hypothetical letters, expression of specific emotions, lists, responses to reading material, notes and responses to an audiocassette, and so forth.

Focused writing is more general in content. It is used when a counselee may not be able to respond at length to a particular problem. He may only be able to respond to general dynamics regarding an issue. The writing response may stay with an assigned area, or it may wander into various other areas.

The benefit of focused writing is that it capitalizes upon the particular issues the counselee may be feeling personally. It allows for more freedom and resourcefulness. These can be very beneficial qualities in responding to a problem. In focused writing the pastoral counselor simply asks for a response to a general assignment. A theme, sentence, phrase, or single Scripture passage may be used for the focus of the writing. Though general, the topic still relates to the particular problem the counselee is dealing with.

The pastoral counselor can adopt study guides and materials for writing assignments or develop materials for each counselee. The process of developing materials for particular counselees does not have to be an exhaustive one. It could range from a simple paragraph of instructions to a list of steps to follow. The following guidelines have been adopted from Waylon O. Ward's book *The Bible in Counseling:*

1. Give specific information and instructions to the counselee.

2. Help the counselee arrive at some insight into what he is experiencing emotionally and spiritually.

3. Specify a particular behavior directed at developing his relationship with God (prayer, Bible reading, etc.).

4. Reinforce insights and concepts developed during the counseling session.

5. Teach the individual how to study the Bible by using specific skills such as reading, written feedback, answering specific questions related to the text, and looking up background information in commentaries and other reference works.

6. Clarify the purpose of the written assignment by stating it clearly and openly at the beginning and ending of the assignment.

If a written assignment is given to a couple, discussion between them generally assists in the effectiveness of the assignment. Individual assignments may be given to each spouse, or they may work on the same assignment together.

Multicultural Counseling

This section addresses concerns for pastoral counseling in a multicultural context. A pastoral counselor may come from another culture. There may be individuals who come to a pastoral counselor from another culture. The pastoral counselor is responsible for responding to the needs of all people, including those from another cultural context. The pastoral counselor may refer the counselee to someone who is more capable of counseling in the cultural context of the counselee. However, the pastoral counselor may also counsel the individual, paying attention to important principles and methodological concerns regarding cross-cultural counseling.

There are many approaches to cross-cultural counseling. The essential outline of this section is an adaptation of concerns expressed by the Association of Multicucultural Counseling and Development, a Division of the American Counseling Association.

The Counselor's Self-Awareness

The pastoral counselor must be aware of his own cultural background, especially his beliefs and attitudes. These are attributes that are almost second nature. They are at the most fundamental level of the pastoral counselor's life. While these are personal, they are also affected by culture. The pastoral counselor should endeavor to decipher which items are more the result of culture. Culturally tempered beliefs and attitudes should be filtered for the counselee in a cross-cultural context.

The pastoral counselor should accumulate as much information as possible about his particular cultural background. This assists in the filtering process just mentioned. It is important to be aware of culturally affected parts of one's life. The pastoral counselor may not be aware of such items until he actively seeks to find out from family history, investigation of cultural customs, and so forth, what may have been a matter of culture in his life.

The pastoral counselor should endeavor to use the information and insight he has gained about his own cultural background as valuable information for cross-cultural counseling. The speech, demeanor, gestures, etiquette, and so forth, of the pastoral counselor are all affected by his multicultural awareness. These adjustments make him a more effective pastoral counselor.

The Counselor's Awareness of the Counselee's Culture

After assessing his own cultural conditioning, the pastoral counselor should actively seek to understand the beliefs and attitudes of the cultural nature of the counselee. Just as he endeavored to discover his own culturally affected beliefs and attitudes, the pastoral counselor should seek the same awareness about the counselee. Beliefs about God, other people, and life in general are all affected by culture.

The pastoral counselor should not only seek to become aware of culturally affected items but also seek to acquire as much of this information as possible. This information may include the history and customs of a particular region of the country or the world. The more information the pastoral counselor is able to acquire about cross-cultural differences, the greater the likelihood that counseling will be more effective.

Counselees may or may not be able to communicate cross-culturally. The pastoral counselor needs to assess their ability to do so. If there is a limited amount of cross-cultural skill, referral may be inevitable. The pastoral counselor can use these skills as a starting place for effective counsel.

Counseling Methods for Cross-Cultural Needs

Certain methods of pastoral counseling are directed at beliefs and attitudes. The pastoral counselor should maintain a fundamental respect for cultural characteristics and differences possessed by the counselee. The pastoral counselor should also be aware of any culturally related practices of the counselee. Further, attitudes are linked to differences in language. The pastoral counselor should endeavor to recognize variances in language.

There are certain pastoral counseling methods directed at knowing about culturally relevant and different aspects. The pastoral counselor should have a knowledge of matters of living that are not as biased by culture. These include faith in Christ, universal attitudes, and fundamental physical needs.

The pastoral counselor should also be aware of barriers which institutions may raise to cultural needs and differences. The pastoral counselor should decipher culturally bound materials and literature that may not be usable in different cultural contexts. The pastoral counselor should also be knowledgeable of family structures, authority structures, and values that are affected by culture.

There are a number of specific tasks which the pastoral counselor should adjust in multicultural counseling. Verbal and nonverbal expressions should be used which are appropriate for a particular cultural context. Pastoral counselors should be especially careful to help the counselee overcome any guilt feelings he may have because of cultural differences.

Being able to effectively refer counselees is another important cross-cultural counseling skill when the pastoral counselor has reached the limits of his ability to help the counselee. This is part of the overall skill of being able to identify the limits of the counselor as well as the counselee's limits of cultural adaptability.

Theocentric Priorities in Multicultural Pastoral Counseling

Jesus ministered in a cross-cultural context in John 4. The Samaritan woman was in need of ministry, though she was from a culture different from Jesus' Galilean and Judean background. Jesus was not afraid to initiate the ministry. He emphasized the love and forgiveness of the Father, which are universal themes for all cultures. Jesus appealed to the woman to worship and serve the Messiah—more universal themes. Upon receiving salvation, she was able to communicate the essential message back to the people in her own culture. Even though the woman had previously resisted, citing differences in worship and culture, the gospel overcame these obstacles. Jesus was aware of His position and did not deny the differences. However, He appealed to principles which transcended cultural lines.

It is important to remember the action of God in a multicultural context. Though differences occur in cultures, God himself transcends culture. When the pastoral counselor ministers within the work and will of God, he is also bridging and transcending culture.

Pastoral Counseling Within Groups

Pastoral counseling in the context of groups can be a rewarding experience. The group may be part of a church ministry or a special group organized by the pastoral counselor. Frequently groups have a certain goal or purpose in mind. Groups usually function best when they have a clear goal for each member to participate. This serves to give the group a reason for existence. Clarity of the goal is very important. The most important aspect of the goal and the group-counseling ministry itself is having a theocentric perspective. This section will explore some of the dynamics of pastoral counseling in a group context, especially the maintenance of a theocentric focus.

Be Accepting of People

The pastoral counselor should accept people where they are when they first begin in a group experience. People are frequently on guard emotionally. Acceptance and care by the group leader facilitates openness and dialogue in the group-counseling process. The attention of each group member at the beginning of the process is especially focused on the leader. The leader can set the tone in an effective direction by refusing to label individuals, taking them at face value. An important key is to avoid assumptions about character and background. Simply take a here- and-now position, focusing on the immediate situation of the group.

An important milestone in the group process is trust. Trust is more likely to occur if individuals are convinced that other members of the group are sincere and that the leader especially is genuinely expressing himself. The leader can model such behavior by monitoring his own guardedness. Be open and truthful in expressions. This does not mean extreme or reactionary responses. However, the pastoral counselor should develop the skill of honest expression. This will serve as a catalyst for trust within the group.

Keep Participation Voluntary

Group participants should not feel forced to speak or participate. The pastoral counselor may encourage participation. However, genuine participation can rarely be forced. It requires facilitating the occasion for response and then allowing a person to respond when ready. At times the pastoral counselor may ask a person to partici- pate directly. However, this should be the exception. If there is little or no participation from anyone in the group, the effectiveness potential of the group is greatly reduced.

Issues of trust and openness can be addressed by con- tinually giving positive feedback to individuals. This is a form of the ministry of edification. This does not elimi- nate confrontation. However, confrontation is given in order to help an individual. This is the maintenance of enhancing and edifying feedback. Positive feedback assures a person that he is being understood. Further, he is assured that his contribution and presence in the group is valuable.

Be Aware of the Role and Function of Group Leadership

It is difficult for groups to function without a leader. This relates to the direction and purpose of the group. Without purpose, it is difficult to be effective as a group. Also, without constant affirmation of the positive dynamics of the group, it is difficult to be effective. The purpose and positive dynamics of the group are most efficiently created by a leader.

The leader and the group should mutually agree upon the role the leader should take. The role should relate to the purpose and dynamics of the group. The leader must be careful to maintain this covenant. If there are any adjustments, it is again a matter of mutual agreement by the group.

Maintain Confidentiality

An issue very relevant to group ministry is mutually establishing confidentiality. The group should discuss the reality of confidentiality issues early in the group process. Instructions and agreements about confidentiality should be clear and precise. They should be clear enough to be understood and precise enough to be achievable. Without confidentiality it is very difficult to establish trust and authenticity.

One of the group leader's primary responsibilities is to monitor expression and trust. A group member should not be allowed to demean or violate the character of another member. If there is confrontation, the group leader is responsible for framing that confrontation ultimately in a way that will edify the individuals involved and the group as a whole. Expressiveness must be monitored in light of confidentiality. Without this, trust and the group's effectiveness will be greatly reduced.

Monitor Emotional Balance

At times group members can be very emotional. The pastoral counselor should not manipulate the emotions of group members. However, he can identify levels of reactivity. He should model effective emotions and levels of reactivity. He should also address emotions and reactions that may be detrimental to the person involved and the group as a whole. Emotions can be a powerful tool in group ministry. The pastoral counselor is responsible for assisting the group as a whole in steering their emotions in the most effective way possible.

A major task for the pastoral counselor is monitoring his own emotions. He should not become too reactive or exhibit emotions which may be detrimental to the group as a whole. Awareness and monitoring of one's own emotions is an important modeling process. It allows other group members to learn from the practice of the leader.

Begin With a Theocentric Focus

Clarifying the goals of the group from a theocentric perspective is a must. The pastoral counselor should seek the will and action of God in the midst of the group. He should facilitate the group as a whole, seeking the will and action of God for the group. The presence of God is a reality and part of the group. Recognition of His presence is very important in maintaining a theocentric focus. The pastoral counselor should consistently remind the group of the theocentric priorities the group has adopted.

The internal dynamics of the group should come under a theocentric focus. This means that the standard of conduct is the person of Christ himself in the midst of the group. The members of the group are not merely reacting to one another, they are reacting in the presence of Christ. Further, because of their faith relationship, they are reacting directly to Christ as well. The pastoral counselor should remind group members of the presence of Christ in responding to group dynamics.

Suggestions for Application

The following suggestions are made in order to implement the principles of special methodologies in pastoral counseling:

1. Develop a list of steps to go through whenever it appears that counseling will only be for a short period of time.

2. Explain the format you are using to the counselee, relating your desire to accomplish as much as possible in the limited amount of time you have.

3. Maintain a specific focus on one particular problem you are trying to assist the counselee with.

4. Clarify the work of God in the midst of the brief process. Try to specify the way in which you believe the Lord is working. You might consider sharing that conviction with the counselee.

5. Use written assignments from the very beginning of the counseling process.

6. Specify a designated time for written assignment to be done. The time can be mutually agreed upon between the pastoral counselor and the person, couple, and/or family being counseled. The particular time chosen is not as important as maintaining a continuing commitment to that time. If the chosen time does not work out, the pastoral counselor should assist in the selection of a time that will work.

7. Select in advance resources such as study guides and Bible studies that would be good written assignments. Having these available when needed is very important.

8. Do not expect perfect adherence to written homework. It will be work for the counselee. Be an encourager. Any improvement and accomplishment of assignments is a positive sign. If the counselee is unwilling to complete assignments or provides a lot of excuses for not completing assignments, it is a possible indication that he is stuck in emotions and not moving effectively toward behavioral change.

9. Thoroughly assess and review your own cultural background as a pastoral counselor.

10. Analyze those aspects of your counseling methods such as gestures, expressions, or perceptions which may be culturally related.

11. Conduct a thorough analysis of the cultural background of the counselee. Note any particular practices, beliefs, or family structures that may be relevant to cultural issues.

12. Feel free to ask counselees how you might communicate with them in a cross-cultural way.

13. Try to learn at least some of the native language of a cross-cultural counselee.

14. Develop a set of goals and guidelines for the group.

15. Mutually agree with the group about whatever policies and goals are adopted.

16. Clarify the theocentric dynamics occurring in the group.

17. Mutually agree with the group about the role of group members and especially the role of the group leader.

Chapter 12

PASTORAL COUNSELING AND PROFESSIONAL ISSUES

Ethics in Pastoral Counseling

The pastoral counselor must have a clear sense of identity about his role. Various issues to identify include the kind of counseling provided, the kinds of counselees to be helped, and the setting in which counseling ministry takes place. These issues determine the kind of counsel given.

The basic theology about the role of the counselor is important. This book has advocated a theocentric approach. Whatever approach the counselor adopts, he must be ready to explain and defend it. The role of the counselor in the setting of the church and/or private practice must be clear. He should also be ready to explain this role as well.

Responsibility to the Client and the Institutions Served

The pastoral counselor is responsible for the welfare

of the counselee and any sponsoring institution he counsels in. The rights of the counselee include privacy, integrity, and health. These must be respected. The pastoral counselor may counsel in a counseling institution or perhaps in a church setting. This would include a pastor who does a considerable amount of counseling in a church. These institutions are founded on general and specific principles and criteria. The counselor must honor and respect these as much as possible.

If an institution requires a rejection of Christ by the counselor, he must consider his role with the institution. The pastoral counselor must find out the requirements of the church or institution and seek to honor them.

Professional Associates

There are frequently associates within an institution or from other institutions that a pastoral counselor may work with. In a counseling institution these would include other counselors and staff members. In a church these would include the pastoral, counseling, and clerical staff. The pastoral counselor must honor the expertise of these individuals. He must conduct himself in a way that complements the effectiveness of these other individuals.

Qualifications

The pastoral counselor must not claim to have qualifications he does not have. He must not claim to be "certified" without proper credentials from a certifying agency. Whatever credentials a pastoral counselor has he may, and should, claim. For example, if he is a credentialed minister who counsels, he may present himself as a minister who counsels. The primary professional identity should be the one most used. This is the identity for which he is most qualified through certification, credentials, and education. He should not claim a specialty if he does not have the background or experience for that specialty.

Fees

A pastoral counselor may or may not charge a fee. The presence or absence of fees do not necessarily reflect upon the quality of counseling. Whether in private counseling practice, a clinical setting, or a church, fees are appropriate. However, the pastoral counselor must be sure that he is aware of any local or state governmental and professional statutes pertaining to fees. The pastoral counselor must have liability insurance because fees for service create an even greater professional liability. Information regarding fees may be secured through state governmental agencies that certify counselors. Local business agencies should also be contacted if a fee structure is established.

If the pastoral counselor is affiliated with a church counseling ministry, the church is liable for the delivery of services attached with the fees. Many times a church may provide counseling as part of the ministry of the church, accepting fees on a freewill-offering basis. Fees in a private or church counseling ministry must respect the financial status of those being counseled. They must not place an undue burden upon the counselee.

Intimacy

The pastoral counselor must be aware of the sensitivity of the counseling relationship. Any practice or affection shown related to sexual intimacy is strictly unprofessional and forbidden. It is a breach of professional and legal conduct to disrespect the counselee in this way. The pastoral counselor must respect the counselee at all times and not seek to engage in activities that may even appear to be sexually suggestive.

Stereotyping and Discrimination

Biases including race, age, disability, ethnicity, and gender must be avoided by the pastoral counselor. Pastoral counseling must be viewed as a public ministry, endeavoring to meet the needs of as many individuals as possible. The pastoral counselor must not stereotype individuals but allow the love and wisdom of God to guide him in honoring the counselee.

Insurability

The pastoral counselor must insure himself if he continues to expand his counseling ministry. Liability insurance, protecting the counseling practice and any church involved, is very important. Some church liability policies will include counseling ministries of the church. Other liability policies will cover the pastoral counselor as an individual. If the primary professional identity of the pastoral counselor is that of a minister—that is, his ministerial certificate is the primary form of identity that he uses in ministry—he would be insured under the church's liability policy. Even with ministerial certification as one's identity, the minister may want to carry a personal liability policy for counseling, especially if the local church's liability policy appears inadequate. However, if his primary identity is as a counselor, then counselor liability insurance must be secured. The idea that ministers should carry liability insurance is a relatively new one. However, it is increasingly becoming a must in the counseling world.

The Counseling Relationship

Obligation to the Counselee

The pastoral counselor carries an obligation for the welfare of the counselee. Whenever the counselee comes to the pastoral counselor for assistance, the counselor must assume a reasonable measure of responsibility for the welfare of the counselee. The counselor is not neutral. If there is a need on the part of the counselee, the counselor must address that need. If the pastoral counselor is not equipped to meet that need, he should refer the counselee to a resource that could meet that need.

Properly Informing the Counselee

The pastoral counselor has the responsibility before counseling begins to properly inform the counselee of the goals and methods that the counselor will endeavor to use. This avoids any misrepresentation or misinterpretation of the intent or practice of the counselor. This can be done through printed literature or a brief time of orientation. The pastoral counselor should use this opportunity to clarify the roles each of them will play. Further, this allows for clarification of what the counselee can expect from the counseling relationship.

Referrals

The pastoral counselor should have a system of referrals. When the counselor feels there is an area of counseling that lies outside his expertise, he should be prepared to refer the counselee to another counselor or resource. This is especially true of specialty areas of counseling such as abuse and drug and alcohol rehabilitation. The pastoral counselor should be prepared ahead of time with referrals in the community, including law enforcement, medical personnel, and other counselors.

Consultation

A pastoral counselor has the privilege to consult with other counselors about a particular counselee. However, the pastoral counselor must notify the counselee of this right and responsibility ahead of time. This will assure the counselee that as much help as possible will be used in their particular situation. However, even when consulting with another colleague, a pastoral counselor must keep the identity of a counselee confidential.

Culturally Relevant

A pastoral counselor is obligated to provide culturally relevant care. If there is a difficulty in communicating cross-culturally with a counselee, the pastoral counselor must provide resources for the counselee that are more culturally relevant. These resources may include other counselors, pastors, written materials, and group ministry.

Confidentiality

A pastoral counselor is obligated professionally and legally to maintain strict confidentiality about the counseling relationship. This includes the content of the counseling as well as the very fact that an individual has come for counsel. In other words, confidentiality should be such that the pastoral counselor should not even reveal that a particular person has seen him for counseling.

Privileged Communication

Privileged communication identifies the ownership of the content of a counseling relationship. The content of counseling is considered the property of the counselee. The counselor must secure permission from the counselee before any information about the counseling is released. The pastoral counselor may have access and record of the content of the counseling; however, the counselee is the only one authorized to grant permission for that information to be used in any way.

Duty to Warn

The pastoral counselor has a duty to warn someone who may be endangered, whether it would be the counselee or someone that the counselee has threatened. This particularly applies to specific threats made upon that individual. The side of caution must be taken. If the counselee has made a threat about a particular person, the pastoral counselor should immediately inform the counselee of the counselor's obligation to warn that person. This would place the counselee on notice that confidentiality may not be maintained in this matter. The duty to warn takes precedence.

Reporting to Governmental Authorities

The pastoral counselor is obligated to secure necessary information from state authorities about his obligation to notify them of certain counseling cases. The most notable of these would be cases involving violence, espe-

258 • Scriptural Counseling: A God-Centered Method

cially child abuse. The best source of information is the state agency assigned to certify counselors. These agencies are usually located in the capital city. The pastoral counselor is obligated to abide by statutes which require notification of such cases.

Record Keeping

The pastoral counselor must maintain adequate records. The records should be sufficient enough to recall the occasion and content of each counseling session. Record-keeping systems must be properly secured at all times. No one but the pastoral counselor or someone directly designated by him should have access to these records. The records may include a log and individual file on each counselee. Other systems may be more extensive. However, security of the records cannot be overstated.

Pastoral Counseling and Referral Issues

Welfare of the Individual, Couple, or Family

The primary concern when making referrals is maintaining a theocentric perspective regarding the welfare of the individual, couple, or family. This represents a twofold concern: God's direction in the proper decision and assuring that the decision to refer is in the best interest of the counselee. Two major concerns regarding welfare are health and protection. Especially in cases of extreme physical abuse, referral is highly recommended, even if not mandated by state agencies and laws.

Additional Training and Resources for the Counselee

Referral may be necessary because the counselee

needs additional training and resources beyond the ability and availability of the pastoral counselor. If the need exists on the part of the counselee, the pastoral counselor is obligated to assist the counselee in securing those resources. The burden for using those resources is upon the counselee. The responsibility of the counselor does not necessarily extend to providing means of support such as finances for counseling or other services. However, the counselor must make the counselee aware of the availability of specific resources.

Preparation for the Possibility of Referral

If a pastoral counselor feels that referral may be a possibility, he should make the counselee aware of the possibility early in the counseling process. Preparing the counselee for the referral is important. The pastoral counselor becomes the spiritual provider and resource during the referral. Proper preparation is a key to fulfilling this role effectively.

Acceptance of the Idea of Referral

The pastoral counselor can serve a vital ministry by assisting the counselee and family with the idea of referral. Frequently there may be apprehension or resistance to referral. Generally, the responsibility to accept referral is the counselee's. However, a referral may be highly recommended, or in cases such as abuse it may be mandated by state agencies and laws.

The pastoral counselor may assume the primary role of assisting the counselee in adjusting to the new circumstances of the referral. The new referral will probably mean a new set of demands and relationships. The effectiveness of the referral rests in part with the effectiveness of the transferal process.

Monitoring the Emotional and Spiritual Condition of the Counselee

Two areas that may be particularly impacted by referral are the emotions and the personal spiritual devotion of the counselee. The counselee may feel hurt or rejected because of the referral. The pastoral counselor can assure the person of his continuing presence and input in the process. Further, he can frame the referral as a very important part of the helping process. A counselee may also feel spiritually dejected because of the referral. This is why a theocentric focus is important. The pastoral counselor can interpret the referral as part of their faith commitment in seeking the will of God for this particular problem.

Informing the Counselee

The counselee has a right to know about the referral. The pastoral counselor should not hide the need for referral. Consulting with family members, friends, and associates but not with the counselee regarding the referral can be detrimental to the counseling relationship. It is a basic issue of trust. Further, the basic decision regarding referral lies most specifically with the counselee. The effectiveness of the referral is helped by maintaining this important process of notification.

Knowing About the Referring Agency or Person

The counselee has a need to know about the agency or person to whom he is being referred. Whether it is a public health agency, a counseling clinic, a church, or private counselor, the counselee needs to know as much as possible about the referral. The background, fees, and history all need to be clearly communicated to the counselee. The pastoral counselor is responsible for the accurate transmission and interpretation of this information. The pastoral counselor is not responsible for the effectiveness of the agency or person; however, he is responsible for accurately and appropriately informing the counselee about the referral.

Confidentiality and Reporting

The level of confidentiality in referral should be clearly stated to the counselee. Whether the pastoral counselor feels that no information or a lot of information should be shared with the referral, permission must be granted by the counselee. It is best if this is in written form. It is appropriate to simply refer the counselee to the person or agency without any accompanying information. The agency or person is responsible for its own assessment and should be prepared to assume this responsibility.

Involvement in the Process

Whenever possible, the counselee should be included in the process of selecting and deciding upon a referral. Several options can be presented to the counselee whenever possible. This emphasizes that the counselee is ultimately responsible for the actual decision about referral. The pastoral counselor's role is as a facilitator and shepherd in the process.

A Poor Referral

A poor referral may be more harmful than no referral.

Therefore, when a referral is necessary, be sure that it is a good one. Some questions to ask regarding a referral agency or private practitioner are included in the following list, which is an adaption from Charles Kemp's book *A Pastoral Counseling Guidebook.*

1. What is its background?

2. Is there a sponsor for the individual, clinic, or agency?

3. What are the primary and secondary means of support?

4. What kind of counselees will they accept?

5. What is the fee structure?

6. What kind of methodology is used?

7. What kind of qualifications does the staff have?

8. How soon are services available?

9. What opinion do other professionals have regarding the institution and staff?

10. What affiliations and certification do the institution and staff have?

11. What do former counselees say about the person or agency?

12. How can the effectiveness of the person or agency be verified?

13. To whom is the person or agency accountable?

Follow-up on a Referral

Before the actual referral is made, arrange for some means of follow-up. The pastoral counselor can either check with the referral or with the counselee. Regardless of the method of follow-up, the counselee should be notified ahead of time about the pastoral counselor's intentions regarding follow-up.

Suggestions for Application

The principles of ethics and referral in pastoral counseling must serve as a practical guide. The following suggestions help to apply these principles:

1. Find a system of record keeping that works best for you. Be sure to keep the records of each counselee secured and confidential.

2. Remember, even the fact that you are counseling someone should be a matter of confidentiality. The counselee has the privilege of telling others that he is being counseled. However, the pastoral counselor himself does not have that open privilege.

3. Print certain guidelines to assist counselees in understanding your goals in pastoral counseling ministry.

4. Clarify your primary professional identity. Then consistently present your counseling to others in the context of that identity, not overestimating or underestimating the abilities and experience you have as a pastoral counselor.

5. Develop a list of individuals and agencies ahead of time to have available when the need arrives for referral.

6. As a part of your regular orientation, notify counselees regarding your general policy about referral when you first meet with them for counseling.

7. Approach referral as a ministry.

8. Develop a relationship with other colleagues in ministry and the helping professions with whom you can consult regarding the need for referral. This kind of consultation is a good practice to follow in most cases of referral.

9. Take follow-up seriously. The pastoral counselor has a responsibility to at least monitor the level of care the counselee received from the referral.

Bibliography

Adams, Jay E. *How to Help People Change: The Four-Step Biblical Process*. Grand Rapids: Zondervan, 1986.

___. *Shepherding God's Flock: A Handbook on Pastoral Ministry, Counseling, and Leadership*. Grand Rapids: Zondervan, 1974.

___. *A Theology of Christian Counseling: More Than Redemption*. Grand Rapids: Zondervan, 1979.

Augsberger, David. *Pastoral Counseling Across Cultures*. Philadelphia: Westminster, 1986.

Berkley, James D. *Called Into Crisis: The Nine Greatest Challenges of Pastoral Care*. Waco: Word, 1989.

Carkhuff, Robert R. *The Art of Helping VII*. Amherst, Mass.: Human Resource Development Press, 1993.

Cobble, James F. *Faith and Crisis in the Stages of Life: Adult Development and Christian Growth*. Peabody, Mass.: Hendrickson, 1985.

Crabb, Lawrence J., Jr. *Basic Principles of Biblical Counseling*. Grand Rapids: Zondervan, 1975.

___. *The Marriage Builder: A Blueprint for Couples and Counselors*. Grand Rapids: Zondervan, 1982.

Evans, C. Stephen. *Wisdom and Humanness in Psychology: Prospects for a Christian Approach*. Grand Rapids: Baker, 1989.

Gerkin, Charles V. *Widening the Horizons: Pastoral Responses to a Fragmented Society*. Philadelphia: Westminster, 1986.

Gilbert, Marvin, and Raymond T. Brock, eds. *The Holy Spirit and Counseling: Theology and Theory.* Peabody, Mass.: Hendrickson, 1985.

___. *The Holy Spirit and Counseling: Principles and Practice.* Peabody, Mass.: Hendrickson, 1988.

Hauerwas, Stanley. *Suffering Presence: Theological Reflections on Medicine, the Mentally Handicapped, and the Church.* Notre Dame, Ind.: Notre Dame Press, 1986.

Hesselgrave, David J. *Counseling Cross-Culturally: An Introduction to Theory and Practice for Christians.* Grand Rapids: Baker, 1984.

Hiltner, Seward. *Pastoral Counseling: How Every Pastor Can Help People to Help Themselves.* Nashville: Abingdon Press, 1976.

Hoehn, Richard A. *Up From Apathy: A Study of Moral Awareness and Social Involvement.* Nashville: Abingdon Press, 1983.

Holifield, E. Brooks. *A History of Pastoral Care in America: From Salvation to Self-Realization.* Nashville: Abingdon Press, 1983.

Jones, Stanton L., and Richard E. Butman. *Modern Psychotherapies: A Comprehensive Christian Appraisal.* Downers Grove, Ill.: Intervarsity Press, 1991.

Kemp, Charles F. *A Pastoral Counseling Guidebook.* Nashville: Abingdon Press, 1971.

Kennedy, Eugene. *Crisis Counseling: An Essential Guide for Nonprofessional Counselors.* New York: Continuum, 1981.

Kern, Roy M. *Lifestyle Scale*. Coral Springs, Fla.: CMTI Press.

Kern, Roy M., E. Clair Hawes and Oscar C. Christensen. *Couples Therapy: An Adlerian Perspective*.

Kottler, Jeffrey, and Diane S. Blau. *The Imperfect Therapist: Learning From Failure in Therapeutic Practice*. San Francisco: Jossey-Bass, 1989.

L'Abate, Luciano. Programmed Writing: *A Self-Administered Approach for Interventions With Individuals, Couples, and Families*. Pacific Grove, Calif.: Brooks/Cole, 1992.

___. *Systematic Family Therapy*. New York: Brunner/Mazel, 1986.

LaHaye, Tim and Beverly. *Spirit Controlled Family Living*. Old Tappan, N.J.: Power Books, 1978.

Maston, T.B. *The Bible and Family Relations*. Nashville: Broadman, 1983.

Matheny, Kenneth B., William L. Curlette, David W Aycock, James L. Pugh, and Harry F. Taylor. *Coping Resources Inventory for Stress Manual*. Atlanta, Ga,: Health Prisms, 1989.

McBurney, Louis. *Counseling Christian Workers*. Waco: Word, 1986.

McSwain, Larry L., and William C. Treadwell. *Conflict Ministry in the Church*. Nashville: Broadman, 1981.

Meier, Paul D., Frank B. Minirth, Frank B. Wichern, and Donald E. Ratcliff. *Introduction to Psychology and Counseling: Christian Perspectives and Applications (2nd ed.).* Grand Rapids: Baker Book House, 1991.

Merrill, Dean. *Clergy Couples in Crisis: The Impact of Stress on Pastoral Marriages.* Waco: Word, 1985.

Oates, Wayne. *An Introduction to Pastoral Counseling.* Nashville: Broadman, 1959.

Oden, Thomas C. *Pastoral Counsel.* New York: Crossroad/Continuum, 1989.

Oglesby, William B., Jr. *Biblical Themes for Pastoral Care.* Nashville: Abingdon Press, 1980.

Osterhaus, James P. *Counseling Families: From Insight to Intervention.* Grand Rapids: Zondervan, 1989.

Puryear, Douglas A. *Helping People in Crisis.* San Francisco: Jossey-Bass Publishers, 1979.

Rekers, George A. *Counseling Families.* Waco: Word Publishers, 1988.

Swihart, Judson J., and Gerald C. Richardson. *Counseling in Times of Crisis.* Waco: Word, 1987.

Ward, Waylon O. *The Bible in Counseling.* Chicago: Moody Press, 1977.

Wheeler, Mary S., Roy M. Kern and William L. Curlette. *BASIS-A Inventory.* Highlands, N.C.: TRT Associates, 1994.

Willimon, William H. *Clergy and Laity Burnout.* Nashville: Abingdon Press, 1989.

Wright, H. Norman. *Crisis Counseling: Helping People in Crisis and Stress*. San Bernardino, Calif.: Here's Life, 1985.

___. Marital Counseling: *A Biblical, Behavioral, Cognitive Approach*. San Francisco: Harper and Row, 1981.